PROCLAMATION COMMENTARIES

**Second Edition
Revised and Enlarged**

Gerhard Krodel, *Editor*

D1040011

Frederick W. Danker

FORTRESS PRESS   PHILADELPHIA

To Martha H. Dreyer
and all other benefactors of
Christ Seminary—Seminex
who encouraged scholarly enterprise

Library of Congress Cataloging-in-Publication Data

Danker, Frederick W.
    Luke.

    (Proclamation commentaries)
    Bibliography: p.
    Includes index.
    1. Bible. N.T. Luke—Criticism, interpretation,
etc. I. Title. II. Series.
BS2595.2.D36 1987   226'.406   86-45905
ISBN 0-8006-0598-5

2567A87 Printed in the United States of America 1-598

CONTENTS

PREFACE

My early interest in Luke's work took shape with awareness that this evangelist was not only a teacher of the church but a master writer. The work of Henry J. Cadbury contributed much to this conviction, but the impression that Luke's work made on his first-century public needed more full-dress exposure. With the latter in mind, I wrote a commentary on Luke's Gospel, *Jesus and the New Age: A Commentary on the Third Gospel* (St. Louis: Clayton Publishing House, 1972), the first commentary to combine modern literary analysis and historical study in such a way that the contemporary reader is able to sense some of the impact that this Gospel as a totality must have made on its first-century recipients.

Once *Jesus and the New Age* had been substantially revised for a second edition (Fortress Press, 1987), it was imperative to revise what I consider to be an introductory volume to this commentary, namely, *Luke,* Proclamation Commentaries (Fortress Press, 1976.)

A major point made in the earlier edition of both works is the role of Greco-Roman "people of excellence," many of whom were referred to as benefactors, as models for grasping certain aspects of God's communication in connection with Jesus and his followers. Some scholars have asked whether this is an appropriate model for understanding Luke's presentation. To the surprise of many, Luke himself decided the matter in Acts 10:38:

> Benefactor (*euergetōn*) that he was, Jesus went about healing all who were tyrannized by the devil.

Modern studies that focus on the social context for biblical interpretation do not permit evasion of Luke's own statement and the manner in which throughout Luke-Acts, his two-volume work, he interprets Jesus as the uniquely Great Benefactor, who in turn directs the thoughts and energies of his followers into channels of beneficent undertaking. But in response to requests for further evidence of Luke's avowed intention, both of my revised works now include further information about the Greco-Roman cultural environment in which Luke's works took their shape. Since the larger commentary contains more detail on these matters, the user of the present study will find in it further support of the positions here taken.

Greco-Roman society was, in fact, steeped in awareness of the dominant role played by reciprocity. In Plato's *Meno* (96e), Sokrates expresses the common Hellenic understanding that the good people are those who render service and are beneficial to others. Beneficiaries are expected to respond with appropriate recognition and awards. Details concerning this cultural phenomenon are provided, together with translations of numerous Greek documents inscribed on stone, in my *Benefactor: Epigraphic Study of a Graeco-Roman and New Testament Semantic Field* (St. Louis: Clayton Publishing House, 1982).

As used in this book, the English term "benefactor" does not translate any single Greek word, for, as *Benefactor* demonstrates, the Greek language has a large number of terms that form an extensive semantic field. "Benefactor" is therefore an umbrella word or generic term that covers the broad spectrum of manifestations of excellence as perceived in the Greco-Roman world, with reference to both deities and human beings. Such manifestations include especially performance of extraordinary deeds, displays of generosity, and exhibition of exceptional moral and spiritual competence, with emphasis on uprightness (*dikaios* is one of Luke's favorite words) and piety. Not all of these features are necessarily characteristic of every subject.

Even a superficial reading of Luke-Acts will reveal Luke's interest in the theme of beneficence. At Acts 28:2, Luke notes that the people of Malta showed "unusual kindness" (*philanthrōpia*) to the entourage of which he was a part. Similarly Publius extended courteous hospitality (v. 7). Like the women of Luke 8:1–3, the affectionate recipient of Jesus' bounty (7:36–50), and grateful Zacchaeus (19:1–10), the early Christians showed that they had learned the meaning of beneficence (Acts 2:44–47; 4:32–37). And like his counterpart in the Gospel (Luke 7:5) Cornelius emerges in Acts (10:2–4) as a philanthropist in the public sphere. At Acts 24:2–3 Luke parodies the fulsomeness with which heads of state frequently were lauded for real or imagined benefits. Nor are pseudo- or anti-benefactors, that is, those who falsely pose as sponsors of excellence, lacking in Luke's record. Governor Felix left Paul in prison "to do the Jews a favor" (24:27). Herod Agrippa I appears in Acts 12 as a benefactor, some of whose political favors were paid for by the life of James the son of Zebedee and the arrest of Peter. The ultimate pseudo-benefactor, of course, is the devil, who offers Jesus the world (Luke 4:5–7). Much of the attraction that Luke's Gospel must have had for his ancient auditors indeed relates to the dramatic interplay of beneficence and pseudo-beneficence in Luke's description of the ministry of Jesus (the Gospel) and the work that he continues through his followers (Acts). Of special interest is the role played by Pilate in the execution narrative. Pseudo-benefactor that he is, he hands over Jesus, the Great Benefactor, to a pressure group and releases an enemy of society, a non-benefactor (Luke 23:24–25). The word "benefactor" is of Latin origin. Its antonym is "malefactor" (Greek, *kakourgos*). Pilate's ignorance of the dimensions of meaning in this moment of history is displayed in his crucifixion of Jesus between two malefactors (*kakourgoi*, 23:32–33). Later in the day, Jesus declares the beneficence of executive clemency to one of them (23:43).

Together with the frequent references to OT material, the cultural excursions taken in this study thus help the modern reader take account of non-Jewish as well as Jewish perspectives for understanding Luke's Gospel. In an ancillary way, this study and the commentary will assist those who wish to engage in sociological study of Luke's book, a study that cannot be undertaken without attention to details of the type explored in both of these works.

Discussion of the probable authorship of Luke-Acts is available in the companion volume to this study. The work is anonymous, and paucity of data make all assumptions highly speculative. I take the view that the work is written in the 80s of the first century, and that the author used material that was also accessible to Matthew and common to Luke but not found in Mark's gospel. This body of material is ordinarily known as Q. Luke also draws on what appears to be Mark's Gospel as we substantially know it. Besides these two sources he had access to materials called L that are not found either in Matthew or Mark.

I have endeavored to keep technical jargon at a minimum, but I frequently use the word "pandemic," which is derived from the Greek *pas* (*pan,* all) and *dēmos* (people), meaning "for all the people," that is, "general." Benefactors were praised especially for a general public outreach.

Through the beneficence of the Aid Association for Lutherans as displayed in a Distinguished Service Award, I was able to pursue further study of epigraphic data that have assisted me in my interpretation of Luke's work. John A. Hollar of Fortress Press has given me generous and discerning counsel in the course of this revision. Special thanks is due my wife, Lois, for expediting this task of revision by making the first edition of this book available to me in diskette form. I am also grateful to Clayton Publishing House for permission to quote from *Benefactor.* Unless otherwise specified, all translations of non-biblical works are my own. With the exception of renderings that overlap with the Revised Standard Version, translations of biblical passages are also my own.

FREDERICK W. DANKER
Chicago, Illinois
October 18, 1986

Benefactor that he was, Jesus
went about healing all who were
tyrannized by the Devil.

Acts 10:38

"ORDERLY RECITAL"

CHAPTER ONE

THOUGHT AND STRUCTURE

Because of Luke's unusual literary methodology, an interpreter must have an especially firm grasp of his main lines of thought before attempting to understand the smaller units of this evangelist's work. This caution is preeminently important for proclaimers, who are necessarily committed to exploration of portions of texts for liturgical purposes.

Among the odd fortunes of history is the fact that one of Luke's main heroes, Paul, is indirectly responsible for giving his press agent Luke secondary intellectual credentials, especially with reference to his theological acumen. By adapting the literary form popularized by Mark and by drawing parallels between the history of Jesus and the church, with Jesus functioning as prime actor in both parts, Luke disqualified himself as a magisterial authority of the kind expressed in Paul's epistolary style. Conveying an air of complete objectivity, he rarely engages in overt editorial comment. Therefore, to determine how he understood his data in coherent relationship, it is necessary to probe for the nerve centers of his two-volume work, Luke-Acts, with his Gospel as the focal point in this book.

What emerges from a literary analysis of Luke's work is the portrait of an artisan who is master of his material to an extraordinary degree. Rhetorical patterns and diction that find repeated expression begin to function as clues to interpretive and editorial purpose that point to Luke's end product as a remarkable combination of historical data and intellectual penetration.

So skillful is Luke at communication of the various levels of thought in his tradition that like a composer of psychedelic effects he is able to project at one and the same time data that are of interest to a polemicist, to one captivated by the force of moral power, to one mired in a morass of varying opinions, or to one who is just curiously asking: "What was Jesus like? . . . What were some of the things he said? . . . Did he die nobly?"

Luke's writing may also be likened to a television set. From the front one sees a coherent picture. Looking in from the back one sees an arrangement of parts and a mass of variously colored wires. The wires all have their function, and all the functions are interrelated. So it is with Luke's work. Even strands of conflicting viewpoints can help form a unified picture. Failure to understand and appreciate Luke's complex artistry led theologians of the nineteenth century to miss the many dimensions in Luke's portrait of Jesus, with the result that Luke's Jesus ran the hazard of becoming irrelevant to human experience. Studies in recent decades have done much to rehabilitate Luke as a theologian-historian, but at the same time one runs the risk of losing Luke's very "human" dimension. This study is an attempt to stimulate further discussion and research and at the same time, and primarily, provide students and the proclaimers among them with a base for more detailed study of Luke's text.

The evangelist's perspective can be summed up in a phrase: "Christology is ecclesiology, and ecclesiology is Christology." Behind this appraisal lies the axiom that serves as seed-plot for Luke's writing: God is the creator of all, merciful to all, and judge of all. Since all Luke's thought-growth has its roots in such theological soil, in this chapter we shall sketch the main outlines of his thinking in terms of the principal problem he faced and then present a preview of the solutions he proposes.

Problem of Gentile and Jewish Misunderstanding

Gentiles

None of the problems faced by Luke was more challenging than the parochial concepts of God that penetrated the Mediterranean world. Apart from sophisticated intellectuals, prospects for conversion from the Jewish diaspora as well as those from the non-Jewish world would find it difficult to adapt to views that conflicted with their own inherited theological ideas and cultic habits.

Much of Rome's success lay in its ability to overcome parochialism by encouraging subordination of local cult under the interests of Divine Rome (*Dea Roma*). Gradually, after permission was granted by Augustus and Tiberius in select provinces, a fanatical propensity in the East for deification led to widespread cultic recognition of the emperor's person. There was, to be sure, a strong ingredient of political ecumenism in this new trend, but narrow parochial interests found security and a hope for permanence in Rome's administration of the world. A decree of the year 37, from Assus, a city in Asia Minor, praised the beginning of Caligula's reign:

> Inasmuch as the reign of Gaius Caesar Germanicus Augustus, the reign that all humanity has been prayerfully anticipating, has been announced by proclamation, and inasmuch as every city and nation hastens to view our deity, as though the most delightful age had dawned for humanity, therefore, be it *resolved* by the council, by the Romans among us who are engaged in business, and by the Public Assembly of the Assians, to appoint an embassy composed of the most distinguished Romans and Hellenes to visit and rejoice with him and petition him to keep our city in fond remembrance as he promised when he first visited our province in the company of his father Germanicus.[1]

Roman citizens or subjects accustomed to expressions of loyalty of this type would be reared in awe of Rome's control of the fortunes of the greater part of humanity. They would also be concerned about the stability of societal patterns in general, including the institution of slavery in particular.

To one who thought along such lines, declarations of the kind expressed in Luke's Magnificat (1:46–55) or in the Sermon on the Plain (6:17–49) might be construed as either revolutionary threat or as preposterous deception typical of wild-bearded religious fanatics. To one also acquainted with the dramas of Greece and their successors that were played on stages throughout the Mediterranean world, encouragement of humility would suggest servility without potential, for freedom and nobility of person were the themes that captivated theatergoers. Yet the Christian community expected the world to believe the story of a man who died the death of a rebellious slave, who lost his capital city because of the rebellion of its inhabitants, and who had no visible means of political support.

Jews

Unique in the world of cultic devotees were the descendants of Abraham and their adopted family of proselytes. Rome had to recognize that Jews in centuries gone by had learned their lesson so well that no power of tyranny could ever shake their descendants out of fidelity to the provisions of the Shema, "Hear, O Israel, the Lord our God is One Lord" (Deut. 6:4). This God had liberated their ancestors from the land of Egypt and had put Israel under the claim of God for all time, yet with responsibility for the welfare of the nations who were to learn of the uniqueness of Yahweh through Israel's various deliverances.

Reared with profound respect for the law of their fathers and with almost equal respect for the traditions of their religious experts, both lay and official, they would find shocking many of the stories about Jesus' circumvention of sabbath ordinances, his apparent flaunting of traditionally accepted amenities, his words that seemed barbed with arrogance, his chiding of religious superiors, and his general encouragement of what seemed to be social, economic, and religious sedition. The triumphant proclamation of the death of a criminal, pronounced righteous (*dikaios*) by his adherents, not only would seem to be revolt against Rome's interests and disturbing to the delicate diplomatic relations between Romans and Jews, but outright blasphemy to one brought up in an ever-narrowing circle of Deuteronomism. Moreover, an ardent reader of the prophets would find assurance of messianic fulfillment in connection with Jesus a cruel hoax, for promised deliverance had not come as expected. Instead of streaming in worship to Jerusalem, in accordance with prophetic description, Rome had sacked Zion in the year 70, and righteousness was not covering the earth. In short, acceptance of Jesus as Messiah would have meant a revolution in Jewish religion in Luke's time.

Bombarded by pleas to retain traditional loyalties, threatened by ostracism from their own families, not to speak of their neighbors and business associates, and barraged by mouthpieces for the old orders, whether of Jewish or imperial allegiance, Christians would find themselves subject to division under the confusing rhetoric of personality cultists. Ultimately, in Luke's judgment, Christianity would risk losing its continuity with the history of God's chosen people Israel and being irrelevant in history's further course. To meet this crisis of faith Luke used as the framework of his communication a cosmopolitan theological approach that had found expression in the Hellenized literature of Israel, including the apocrypha.

Way to Unity

Beginning with his basic view of God's supremacy from the beginning of creation to the end of time, Luke found the way to unity out of all the diversity within his community and within his theological sources. Running as a main thread through all the Scriptures and associated literature was the theme of God's merciful benefactions. The problem confronting Luke was communication of a proclamation that would have its roots in Israel's past, yet speak meaningfully to contemporaries in the Greco-Roman world.

Any classic offers a variety of entrance points for exploration of its meaning, and this is certainly true of Luke's work. If there appears to be a blockade at some point because of a cultural gap between the data of the text and the world of the interpreter, there is usually a bypath along which Luke's presentation can be grasped. At the outset he signals his ability to reach both Jews and Greco-Romans. The prologue to his Gospel is elegant, but thereafter he writes in the style of Greek translations of the Hebrew Bible. But he can count on Greco-Roman auditors to appreciate the antiquity of the Jewish Scriptures, and the quaint style of his work would invite their further attention. Both Jew and non-Jew would therefore bring to Luke's work their cultural experiences, which would in turn serve as a hermeneutical medium for understanding his story. Luke could count on Jews to recognize his allusions to stories and themes that belonged to the very soul of Jewish identity, and by the manner in which he organized and expressed his material he could invite his Greco-Roman auditors to use features of their cultural inheritance as models for understanding what would be appreciated along other routes by Jews. It is not too helpful, therefore, to think narrowly in terms of what some have called "Luke's community." Rather, his work suggests a variety of publics, among them especially Greco-Romans, some acquainted with Jewish tradition and others not.

In part 2 of this study we shall explore the principal ways in which Greco-Romans might have found a means of entry into Luke's work. This is not to deny that Jews had parallel cultural experiences, but to demonstrate that Luke's literary artistry provided avenues for non-Jewish appreciation even of heavily loaded Jewish material. Since recognition of heads of state and civic-minded people was a dominant cultural phenomenon, especially in the eastern part of the Roman Empire, we will sketch the manner in which Luke's presentation of Jesus would be understood in terms of the Greco-Roman ideal of a person of exceptional merit and noted especially for beneficence (chap. 3). Through a specific aspect of this cultural model, the "endangered benefactor," the suffering and death of Jesus are subject to new inquiry. Greco-Roman acquaintance with the theme of reversal in both literary works and proverbial wisdom offered non-Jews still another route into the heart of Luke's work. And this avenue is traced in chapter 4, which deals with the rise-and-fall and fall-and-rise strain in Luke-Acts.

Since Luke emphasizes the role of the Hebrew Scriptures in the formation of his work (see Luke 24:27, 44), it is evident that Jewish experience offered a hermeneutical medium that made entry into the meaning of Luke's work possible also for Jews. Especially significant is the fact that Luke shows Jesus reciting three passages from Deuteronomy at Luke 4:4, 8, 12. Part 3, therefore, discusses names and titles of Jesus, with focus on Israel's mission as Servant and God's way of dealing with "hardness of heart."

Finally, part 4 helps the student enter Luke's work through a brief study of his perception of ethics and the resources he provides for Christian proclamation that aims to be in continuity with the world and the people of God in Luke's time.

Through a number of avenues, then, this study affords access to meanings in Luke's work. The following outline serves as an initial instrument for exploration of his Gospel.

Theme and Structure of Luke's Gospel

At Luke 1:1–4 the evangelist informs us of the importance of his undertaking, and from Acts 1:1 we derive Luke's own statement of the scope of his first volume: "an account of all that Jesus began to do and to teach." Some kind of continuation in harmony with his deeds and words is here anticipated, and Acts 1:8 summarizes the outline: "You shall receive power when the Holy Spirit comes over you, and you will be my witnesses in Jerusalem, throughout Judea, in Samaria, and on to the farthest reaches of the earth" (Luke 24:45–47).

But it is one thing to define content, and another to establish the main thread that connects the items contained. To arrive at the coordinating thought it is methodologically necessary to distinguish theme from subsidiary aims and purposes that are to be achieved through exposition of a specific theme. Especially is such distinction necessary in the case of an avowed two-volume work, for the aims of the author in the two parts may be varied, but through all the parts he might well be pursuing one principal theme.

Theme

If one had asked Luke to state in one clause what he considered to be the unifying thread in his two volumes, he might well have replied:

> **Despite defections, Israel's mission as Servant of the Lord and benefactor to the world finds fulfillment under the endowment of the Spirit through Jesus and his followers.**

It will be noted that this formulation of the theme of Luke-Acts first of all takes into account Luke's own statement of content in his two books. As we will demonstrate, there are numerous data that point to servanthood as a primary ingredient in Luke's conceptions. These data suggest that through traditions associated with Isaiah's point of view (e.g., Isa. 61:1-2; Luke 4:18-19) Luke was able in his Gospel to interpret Jesus as a prophet of mighty deed and word both to Jews and non-Jews in the Greco-Roman world, which was well acquainted with official benefactors. Israel as Servant of the Lord was to attract Gentiles to the knowledge of Yahweh, who is the Supreme Benefactor. Acts presents Jesus as an imperial figure who associates the apostles and St. Paul with himself in the achievement of Israel's mission.

Second, this statement of the theme takes into account Luke's intimate conjunction of the Holy Spirit with the activity of both Jesus and the church, a connection that is integral to the figure of the Servant in Isaiah.

Third, this formulation takes into account Luke's apparent preoccupation with the failure of Israel's religious leadership to grasp the identity of Jesus. It also does justice to his associated interest in christological and eschatological-apocalyptic issues.

Fourth, it accounts for Luke's interest in the ethical integrity of the Christian community, which through repentance and faith carries out its Servant mission.

Fifth, it accounts for the relative paucity of treatment of the development of the early church, of its problems, and of the lives of the apostles; and it does justice to the ending of Acts.

Sixth, it takes into account theological contradictions in Luke's work.

Seventh, it puts subsidiary aims, such as antignostic thrust, apologetic-evangelistic interest, validation of Paul's ministry, political apologetic, or endeavor to account for delay of the Parousia, into clearer perspective.

Throughout Luke's work, then, there runs a basic pattern of promise-fulfillment and rejection-success. God, Supreme Benefactor, reaches out to the world at the time appointed through the rejected Servant-Benefactor Jesus and through the Benefactor-Servant-Community, Israel-the-Church.

An Outline of Luke's Gospel

Prologue (Luke 1:1–4)

In the prologue Luke informs his public through Theophilos that so far as he is concerned theology has to do with the present situation in which the church found itself. That present moment, around the years 80–85, was the climax of history, but there was confusion about its shape. Luke does not question the accuracy of the many recitals in circulation, but it is one thing to record anecdotes and another to sort them and bring them all into meaningful relationships. This last will be Luke's contribution to history. Then Theophilos and whatever public Luke enjoys will have some certainty (v. 4), after their bewilderment which was generated by a mass of conflicting claims and counterclaims that were based on the many different recitals, which apparently included Mark and Q.

Luke informs his public in Acts 1:1 that he endeavored in his first volume to relate "everything that Jesus began to do and to teach." By the word "everything" Luke certainly does not mean every item he came across, but a fair sampling of what is in circulation about Jesus, and with emphasis on his objectivity in executing the task. As our analyses will demonstrate, Luke did not hesitate to include sayings and stories that at first sight would be prejudicial to his own thematic interests. Rather than completeness, fairness in appraisal is one of Luke's primary concerns.

Part 1: Beginnings (Luke 1:5 – 2:52)

In his first two chapters Luke introduces a number of problems and themes which come up for solution and discussion in the rest of his work. Most crucial was the question of the interrelationship of John and Jesus. Mark's omission of a birth narrative and the manner of treatment he accorded John created questions that clamored for answer. Through close association of the births of John and Jesus, Luke was able to parallel their infancies in such a way that the credentials of Jesus are in no way dependent on those of John as an apocalyptic figure. In the Magnificat (1:46–55) Luke presents the theme of reversed fortunes for the lowly and the privileged, a theme that includes acceptance of the Gentiles. The Benedictus (1:68–79) introduces the main christological issues and includes the leading themes of Abrahamic promises, of Davidic-messianic dynasty, moral responsibility, and the eschatological motifs of salvation, the Servant's mission, and the expectation of peace. In his initial response to the angel, Zechariah gives expression to the theme of resistance to the divine word. His function as a priest in Jerusalem also gives Luke the opportunity to begin his Gospel in the geographical locale that was the focus of prophetic expectation.

In the annunciation to Mary, the basic christological problem, namely the relation of Davidic hope to the Servant's function as obedient Son of God, comes to the surface, with emphasis on the name Jesus, the decisive confessional name. In the announcement to the shepherds, Luke climaxes his introduction to the christological issue with a concatenation of terms: Savior, Christ, Lord, Son of David ("in David's town"), followed by narration of the circumcision with its emphasis on the name Jesus. Simeon, the righteous (*dikaios*) and devout (*eulabēs*) one (cf. Acts 22:12-16), defines Jesus in terms of the Servant-of-the-Lord motif, but with anticipation of the hardness of heart which the Good News will leave in its wake. But whatever the response may be, Hannah (Anna) attests Jesus as the means of Jerusalem's redemption. And at the age of twelve Jesus identifies with the dynamic christological category —Son of God.

From 1:5—2:52 a clear picture of Luke's method emerges. Through selection and arrangement of his source material, the evangelist openly presents the credentials of Jesus. Gabriel's message, the obedient submission of Mary, and the prophetic voices of Elizabeth, Zechariah, Simeon, and Anna—all attest the identity of Jesus, who at the age of twelve recognizes his unique Sonship of dedicated commitment to his heavenly Father's purpose. Jesus' career as Servant-Benefactor is *no messianic secret*. But Jesus' very commitment to his task will subject him to misunderstanding that will divide both Israel and the world.

Part 2: John the Baptist and Jesus (Luke 3:1-38)

John's proclamation dramatically introduces the prerequisite for Christian existence, for his invitation to repentance is proleptic of all Christian proclamation. His fate is also prophetic of the division that will result from such proclamation. At the same time he announces, in what amounts to a forecast of Pentecost, an endowment of God's people with the Holy Spirit, anticipated by Isaiah for fulfillment of the Servant's mission. The heavenly voice at Jesus' baptism confirms Jesus as the prime agent for achievement of the eschatological hope. With the genealogy (3:23-38) Luke shows that this Jesus, empowered with the Spirit that was promised to Israel's Servant, is the agent of salvation to all humanity. By reevaluating John's prophetic identity in terms of the proclamatory task of God's people, Luke strives to eliminate apocalyptic speculation and thus free the church for responsible action in history—at least "until the times of the Gentiles are fulfilled" (21:24).

Part 3: Outreach to Israel (Luke 4:1-9:50)

In 4:1—9:50 Luke focuses on the identity of Jesus as Servant-Benefactor, mighty in deeds and words. Luke makes a smooth transition through recapitulation of Jesus' receipt of the Holy Spirit. A dramatic conflict is now staged between Jesus-with-the-Holy-Spirit and the Divider-with-the-Evil-Spirit. As exhibited by Jesus' threefold quotation of Deuteronomy against Satan (4:4, 8, 12), the Servant of the Lord emerges from the conflict in commitment to the divine purpose. As such he can identify himself at Nazareth explicitly with the Isaianic Servant (4:18–19; cf. Isa. 61:1–2). But the encounter at Nazareth is also a temptation scene. By juxtaposing the two scenes Luke suggests that all his succeeding presentation of the experiences of Jesus and his followers lies within the perimeters of cosmic conflict, yet he can do this without the disadvantage of commitment to details and vagaries of apocalyptic tradition.

From Acts 2:36 it might be inferred that God first turned Jesus into Christ and Lord through the resurrection, but whatever the primitive tradition might have been, Luke's view is that God gave Jesus as Christ and Lord to the world already at his birth (Luke 2:11), with his identity decreed by the divine word prior to that birth. The Holy Spirit is the crucial factor. Through the power of the Holy Spirit Mary conceives Jesus. Through the power of the same Spirit also the new community takes shape at Pentecost. In brief, Luke affirms that the Holy Spirit documents Jesus as the Anointed One in three aspects: his infancy, his earthly ministry, and his death and resurrection.

Beginning with Luke 4:31, the evangelist in the main follows Mark's outline in his presentation of the deeds and words of Jesus, but a number of variations point to distinctive emphases. Quite obvious is Luke's inclusion of the Sermon on the Plain (6:17–49), which provides him with an opportunity to reinforce some of his principal sub-themes: (1) contrast of the lowly and the mighty; (2) inevitability of persecution because of the Name that causes division; (3) revision of societal standards; (4) divine paternal mercy as model for Christian response; (5) recognition of constant need of repentance; (6) sincerity vs. hypocrisy; (7) recognition of the Lordship of Jesus against all competing claims.

In distinction from Mark, who has the story about Beelzebul before the parable of the sower, Luke puts the story (11:14–28) back to back with a contrasting series of sayings, whose main theme is the Holy Spirit (11:1–14). This shift enables Luke to link together a series of recitals whose dominant message is "hear the word of God and keep it" (that is, respond in faith and obedience), a point firmly made in the parable of the sower (8:4–15) and associated sayings (vv. 16–21).

At 9:18 Luke moves immediately from Mark 6:44 to the content of Mark 8:27. This omission expedites an association of Peter's confession with the feeding of the five thousand, and the juxtaposition in turn provides a link with the recital of the transfiguration, thus permitting easy transition to the next phase of Jesus' activity, the journey to Jerusalem. At the same time, the concentration of christological motifs displays the unity in Luke's theological conception, and the feeding narrative anticipates the apostolic continuation of Jesus' benefactions (see Acts 4:4).

Part 4: Journey to Jerusalem (Luke 9:51–19:27)

The second phase of Jesus' activity is presented as a journey to Jerusalem that finds expression in four stages: (1) 9:51–13:21; (2) 13:22–17:10; (3) 17:11–18:30; (4) 18:31–19:27. Having established his main point—Jesus, the Christ, who is destined to suffer, heads for Jerusalem—Luke inserts between Mark 9:41 and 10:13 the long section Luke 9:51–18:14. In anticipation of his journey motif he had already eliminated Mark's specifications of locale (Mark 8:27 = Luke 9:18, Caesarea; Mark 9:30 = Luke 9:43, Jesus goes through Galilee; Mark 9:33 = Luke 9:46, Capernaum), and in the descriptions of Jesus' journey he makes only the one very general reference to "Samaria and Galilee" (17:11). Thereby Luke once more establishes a measure of independence from Mark and gives himself freedom of literary movement. At the same time, the special material he incorporates acquires an aura of timelessness.

1. Luke 9:51–13:21. The recital of the *first stage* of Jesus' journey, with its focus on Samaria and Samaritans, anticipates the mission activity of Acts. Thematically associated are the stress on proper hearing of the word, guidance by the Holy Spirit, and integrity of religious profession, with promise of ultimate triumph of the kingdom.

2. Luke 13:22–17:10. A general sub-theme, "The last shall be first," runs through the *second stage,* with emphasis on problems of entry into the kingdom and on attitudes appropriate to identification with it.

3. Luke 17:11–18:30. In keeping with his view of indiscriminate divine mercy, Luke introduces the *third stage* with the story of the ten lepers, of whom only a Samaritan returns to give thanks. The contrast between him and the nine ungrateful recipients of divine mercy helps define the kind of faith that is necessary for participation in the climactic phase of God's kingdom action.

4. Luke 18:31–19:27. A detailed passion prediction introduces the *fourth stage,* in which Luke's emphasis on repentance is closely related to the problem of kingdom apocalyptic and Jesus' messianic credentials. Salvation is a present reality, for it is realized through the kind of response made by Zacchaeus (19:1–10), which is equivalent to the experience of the blind man in the recital that immediately precedes (18:35–43). The juxtaposition of these two accounts is Luke's way of defining the point made especially in 1:78–79; 2:30; 4:18; 7:22. Without repentance the messianic benefits cannot be realized in either the first or the second phase of the kingdom. Zacchaeus' example cannot, of course, be emulated in precisely the form recorded. Therefore Luke follows up the story about Zacchaeus with a parable on financial transactions,

thereby showing that repentance is essential for participation in the final apocalyptic phase. Through faithful acceptance of any and every responsibility, Jesus' followers carry out the example of Zacchaeus. The climax of the prediction in 18:33, with its reference to ultimate victory, is in chiastic arrangement (inverted parallelism: a b b' a') with the eschatological theme in the parable of the pounds.

Part 5: The Ministry of Jesus in Jerusalem (Luke 19:28–21:38)

Luke's recital of Jesus' entry into Jerusalem (19:28-48) emphasizes that any future aspect of the kingdom develops out of its reality in the present. The phraseology in 19:38 returns Luke's public to the realized apocalyptic of 2:14.

Certainty of Jesus' victory pervades the recitals in 20:1—21:38, a section that serves as introduction to the narrative of final events in Jerusalem.

From Luke's terminating sentences (19:47-48 and 21:37-38) in these two sections, it is evident that he aims to stress the openness and truthfulness of Jesus' instruction. Through the inclusion of the story about the tribute money (20:19-26) he not only reinforces this point (v. 21), but confirms the reality of the kingdom of God in connection with Jesus. To "pay back to God what is God's" means to acknowledge the One who has been made "head of the corner" (v. 17) and exalted "at the right hand" of God (v. 42). Thus the lie recited by the adversary at 4:6 is exposed in a totally fresh dimension. Appropriately, this sequence, with its christological stress, comes to a head in 20:45—21:4 and then in 21:5-36. Jesus, who will be judged worthy of death (anticipated at 19:47; 20:19) will himself be exalted, and there will be especially severe judgment for the phony religionists mentioned in 20:45-47, who will in accordance with the specifications of the Magnificat be humbled, whereas one who, like the widow (21:1-4), lives in committed faith will be exalted. The apocalyptic discourse of 21:5-36 describes the ultimate victory of those who identify with the Son of man. The fact that Jesus assures his disciples that he himself will direct and protect them (vv. 15-19) indicates that the kingdom is present reality, but the final victory phase is still anticipated. For that moment watchfulness is required. The Son of humanity has all power now, but it is important that one be able to "stand before him." Those who can stand before the Son of humanity will indeed escape anything negative that history may throw in their path (v. 36).

Part 6: The Passion Account (Luke 22–23)

Luke's observation that Satan entered into Judas (22:3) at the Passover is not only in continuity with the thematic development that immediately precedes but is also typical of his dramatic sensitivity. In the light of his chief adversary's need to mobilize his resources, the credentials of Jesus are all the more patent. The negative magnifies the positive, and the next hours will open history to "the clash of kings."

In essence, God's anticipated kingdom action is salvation. From Luke's point of view this means the display of divine beneficence, expressed above all in assurance of forgiveness. Jesus is the supreme expression of divine intention toward humanity. Repentance is the port of entry into personal realization of salvation. Climaxing Luke's presentation of the suffering of Jesus is the story of the repentant criminal's (*kakourgos*, malefactor) reception into paradise (23:43), the royal garden, reserved for the righteous. Answering the criminal's indefinite "*when* you enter your kingdom" is the word "*today*." And a centurion reverses the verdict of Caiaphas and Pilate by attesting to the quality of Jesus' life as one of exceptional merit: He glorified God and said that Jesus was upright and innocent (*dikaios*).[2]

Part 7: The Resurrected Lord (Luke 24)

The light of salvation indeed blazed in the darkness (1:78–79) of the apocalyptic moment that spelled "darkness over all the earth" (23:44). But in another sense salvation is yet to be realized, and especially so for Jesus the sufferer. Through his resurrection Jesus experiences the truth of the Magnificat: "God topples the mighty from their thrones and promotes the lowly" (1:52). In anticipation of that exaltation he takes a solemn oath that from the moment of the Passover he "will not drink wine until the kingdom of God comes" (22:18), and in the same hour he promises his disciples that they will be partners in his kingdom (vv. 29–30). Luke 24:26 emphasizes that suffering is the prerequisite for glory. In continuity with the conclusion of the Gospel, the first verses of Acts picture Jesus and the apostles in close association, in preparation for the strategic campaign of the New Age (Acts 1:3–4). The kingdom assured by Jesus in Luke 22:18, 29–30 has arrived (cf. Acts 10:41). There is no further need for the abstinence vowed at Luke 22:18. The kingdom, God's salvation, is reality in connection with Jesus. At no time in all history would God's kingdom activity be more signally demonstrated than in the divine actions relative to Jesus of Nazareth. Jesus' own experience of God's salvation fixes the kingdom within history as a contemporary reality and a model for all deliverances to come. What God does with Jesus is proof of God's beneficent interest in humanity. Therefore salvation is proclaimed in connection with the name of Jesus of Nazareth.

In keeping with the main theme—divine benefaction of forgiveness in connection with the name of Jesus—Luke permits the guilt especially of Jerusalem's leaders to loom large in the passion recital. But this literary datum does not, as is often alleged, emanate primarily from an interest in exculpating Roman government. No one would have taken amiss another nail in Pilate's coffin, and Luke does not hesitate elsewhere to expose corruption in highly placed imperial officialdom. Rather, the accent on Jewish guilt dramatizes the profound depths of divine forgiveness, proclamation of which is to begin at Jerusalem (24:47). The fact that Pilate, a non-Jew, was of a mind to release Jesus makes the crime of Jerusalem's religious establishment all the more reprehensible (Acts 3:13–15). But Luke shares Paul's axiom: "Where sin abounded divine benefaction did much more abound." At the same time, of course, Luke shows that Christians deserve imperial recognition as a group that does not prejudice Rome's interests. It is no accident therefore that he is buried by the good (*agathos*) and upright (*dikaios*) Joseph of Arimathea.

CHAPTER TWO

TOWARD THEMATIC UNITY

To animate his theme and structure Luke chose as a base for his Gospel the pattern of an anecdotal chain established by Mark. This meant a minimum of overt intrusion into the text. But to avoid suggestion of a clumsy scissors-and-paste method he had to discover ways of conveying a sense of unity, while at the same time communicating appropriate interpretation for his contemporaries. Therefore he chose to write his Gospel in a style redolent of the Septuagint. This overall formal unity he then complemented with a number of rhetorical devices, some of which permitted him to accommodate even disparate materials, which find resolution in the course of his work.

Parallelism

Luke's favorite rhetorical-structural device is the use of thematically related or contrasting recitals and sayings, either juxtaposed or distributed in his narrative. In most cases the device is obvious; in others more subtle. Doublets and triads are most frequent.

Overt Parallelism

Prominent in Luke 1 and 2 are the annunciations by the angel regarding John and Jesus, the recitals of their births, and the psalms uttered by Mary (Elisabeth?) and Zachariah. Simeon (2:25-35) and Hannah (vv. 36-38) offer a twofold testimony to the redemptive significance of Jesus.

After the incident at Nazareth, Luke retains the healing of Simon's mother-in-law (4:38-39) within the perspective of the exorcism recorded in vv. 31-37. At the same time he introduces one of his main characters, Simon, who heads a thematically integrated series of recipients of mercy in chapter 5. Luke's view of divine beneficence permeates 5:1-11, one of numerous indications of the way in which Luke impresses his own stamp on miracle recitals; Jesus' miracles are benefactions. Simon, self-styled sinner, is the recipient of absolution through the invitation to share in the Servant mission of Jesus. His receipt of forgiveness is paralleled by the paralytic's experience (vv. 17-26). The leper (vv. 12-16) and Levi (vv. 27-29) are typical of religious and social outcasts. Thus the series follows the pattern a b a' b' and reaches its climax in the thematically integrating saying of v. 32 ("I have not come to call the righteous, but sinners to repentance"), which is motivated by the dialogue in vv. 30–31. In partial explanation of the hostile reception accorded the liberalizing message of the Good News, Luke records two illustrations (the patched garment, v. 36; and the appropriate wineskins, vv. 37–38) and, to nail down the meaning, concludes with the explicit saying in v. 39.

Four woes in 6:24–26 balance the four blessings in vv. 20–22, thus forming an introductory pair of sayings. The contents are traditional, but Isaiah 5 and 65 may have stimulated Luke to effect the present arrangement.

In anticipation of the pronouncement in 7:22, which includes a reference to resurrection, Luke relates a story about a slave who is on the point of death (7:1–10) and one about a widow's son who had in fact died (vv. 11–17).

In chapter 9 the thematic link is the question of the eschatological prophet, with emphasis on Elijah and Moses. At vv. 7–9 Herod's perplexity finds expression; vv. 10–17 suggest a page from Elijah's life; and vv. 28–36 finally isolate Jesus from Moses and Elijah.

To further endorse his theme of hearing the word of God, Luke retains the double witness of Solomon's regal visitor (11:31) and the Ninevites, with concluding emphasis on the repentance of the latter. Particularly elegant is Luke's pairing of the tripled woes in 11:42, 43, 44 and 46, 47, 52. To sharpen the point of the parable in 12:35–40, Luke records an alternate form (vv. 42–48).

In keeping with the instruction of the Magnificat, 14:7–11 recommends self-humiliation; vv. 12–14 complement the instruction; and a third illustrative story (vv. 15–24) completes a banquet triad, thereby projecting the social protocol expressed in the two previous recitals within a perspective clearly shaped by the fatuous remark of one of the guests (v. 15).

Two stories with related refrains (15:6–7 and 9:10) lend further perspective to the story of the unwilling brother, which concludes the triad, with a variation of the earlier refrain (vv. 31–32). Since this triad might suggest that divine benefaction clears the road to easy sin, Luke continues in chapter 16 with the story about a crooked steward (16:1–9), which pairs with the story of the rich man and Lazarus (16:19–31). Evidently the story about the crooked steward had led to misunderstanding, and the concluding saying in v. 9 required clarification. Luke removes one level of misunderstanding by emphasizing through a triad of gnomic sayings (vv. 10, 11–12, 13) that the story does *not* aim to encourage misuse of financial trust. On the contrary, Luke points out through criticism of "the Pharisees" that morality in the New Age is to be of the highest order. Some Pharisees may argue that Christian proclamation makes sin easy by lowering kingdom requirements contrary to the manner of John the Baptist, who took sin seriously and demanded repentance (v. 16). In rebuttal of this allegation by the opposition, Luke concludes with a pair of sayings which affirm that Jesus did not undermine Mosaic law (v. 17). Rather, it is certain Pharisees who encourage—through what the evangelist interprets as self-serving casuistry (for example, on divorce, v. 18)—a lower moral standard than do the Christians.

Having demonstrated that forgiveness does not take place without repentance, through the narrative of the rich man and Lazarus, Luke shows how the story of the crooked steward is to be understood in a positive way. Luke's treatment of Paul's conversion suggests how we are to understand the evangelist's technique in connection with several other instances of separated but parallel narratives in Luke and Acts. In the Gospel, Luke twice uses, and in very similar phraseology, a metaphor about light. At 8:16–18 it is used to show that Jesus did not aim to keep Israel from seeing the truth; the blame lies with the hearer. The second, 11:33–36, illustrates the importance of religious integrity. (At 12:2–3 Luke picks up the motif of concealment expressed in 8:17.) The double sending of disciples is of the same rhetorical order. Luke 9:1–6 records the dispatch of the Twelve, followed by the story of the feeding in the vicinity of Bethsaida. Luke 10:1–12 narrates the appointment of the Seventy (-two), this time followed by pronouncement of woe on Bethsaida (vv. 13–14). Acts 4:1–4 and 5:17–20 similarly contain related narratives about imprisonment.

Less Overt Parallelism

Reserved for special discussion are a number of passages whose interpretation depends to some extent on recognition of Luke's method of parallel narration, but one that moves on a deeper conceptual level. Failure to appreciate this more subtle application by Luke of an otherwise obvious rhetorical device has on occasion misled scholars into attributing to Luke artistic and theological inconsistencies of which he is not guilty.

Luke welcomed the tradition of Jesus' Davidic ancestry (Luke 1:26–33), for he was able to make theological capital out of Davidic messianic passages, especially those from the Psalms. But, the nationalistic potential of the tradition had to be put in the larger perspective of Luke's understanding of the Servant. Therefore Luke climactically presents the tradition of Mary's virginal conception (vv. 34–35), with emphasis on the Holy Spirit. Luke 4:16–30 is of primary thematic importance for Luke, and with its stress on Jesus' Spirit-endowment for his Servant mission it complements the recital in vv. 10–15. In the one case, Jesus, led by the Holy Spirit, is tempted by the devil; at Nazareth he encounters the hostility of his townspeople who threaten what Satan specifically succeeds in achieving after finding an ally in Judas (22:3) and in Jerusalem's religious establishment (v. 53). In such manner this pair of narratives is hermeneutically cross-fertile and functions also as an anticipation of one of Luke's motifs, "Behold, we turn to the gentiles" (Acts 13:46). Nor is Luke in this recital unconscious of the dramatic fact that no miracles have yet been done in Capernaum. Therefore he uses the future tense, "you will say," in 4:23 and brings Capernaum into literary orbit immediately at v. 31.

The transfiguration narrative (9:28–36) is matched by a story (vv. 37–43) whose scenery is of a more pedestrian level but which reaches a climax in distinctive phrasing, to the effect that God's function as a benefactor has come to extraordinary expression in the exorcism (v. 43). Apocalyptic conclusions are to be based on recognition of Jesus' words and deeds, not vice versa, affirms Luke through this juxtaposition.

Luke's rationale for linking the recital about Mary and Martha (10:38–42) with the story of the Good Samaritan (10:25–37) finds illumination in his predilection for pairs. To follow the pattern of the Samaritan's response requires constant attention to what in Luke's time would be "the Christian message." The story in 10:38–42 does not pit passivity against action, but motivates activity with receptivity to the Great Benefactor's word. Martha reflects another phase of what Luke understands as the self-righteous legalist; Mary is the potential Good Samaritan.

Luke 11:1–26 embraces a contrasting pair. Divine beneficence manifested in the gift of the Holy Spirit climaxes in vv. 1–13, and vv. 14–26 emphasize the hazard of invasion by demonic forces. The triad in vv. 21–22, 23, and 24–26 is thematically coherent. As often in Luke's use of a series, the last member interprets one or more of the others that precede; in this case the most explicit item is contained in vv. 24–26.

On the other hand, Luke may attach, depending on the context, various meanings to related traditions. In 11:21–22 the strength metaphor is used differently than in 3:16; and the "strong man" refers to one who is overcome in his false sense of religious security by the "stronger one," that is, by a representative of the demonic-counter-kingdom. The second part of the triad (v. 23) evidently means that neutrality toward Jesus is equivalent to a vote for the demonic opposition. The dialogue in 11:27–28 puts the entire sequence in the familiar thematic perspective of "hearing and keeping the word of God," and motivates transition to the subsequent sayings (vv. 29–36), which define such hearing as repentant listening. Similarly, it might be inferred from the singular pronoun (*sou*) in 7:27 and the declaration in 1:17 that a single person, namely Jesus, is the referent. This is the patristic tradition. But Exod. 23:20–21, from which the verse is cited, uses the singular pronoun in reference to Moses' multiple audience and then the second plural in v. 22, followed by mostly singular pronouns and verbs in vv. 23–33. Luke's point is to emphasize the privilege that Israel enjoyed in having John the Baptist as the messenger who came to prepare the way for its Servant-mission.

The story of the rich fool (12:16–21) is a dramatic recitation to the crowds. Its application to the disciples (vv. 22–31) derives from Q. Verse 32 is typical of Luke and is transitional.

Each of the pair of case histories in 13:1–5 terminates with an urgent call to repentance. But the problem of delayed judgment within history, as well as delay of the apocalyptic termination, suggests the need for a further look at divine retribution. The parable in vv. 6–9 not only becomes clear in the light of what precedes it, but human propensity for ignoring warnings that do not appear to materialize finds correction in the light of divine mercy.

Luke's recital of Zacchaeus's conversion (19:1–10) not only puts the toll collector in contrast to the rich man of 16:19–31, but parallels the story of the blind man's experience (18:35–43) and puts salvation into a category that finds repeated expression in Luke's Gospel.

In contrast to Mark 12:38–44, which has two different audiences for the two stories paralleled in Luke 20:45—21:4, Luke has Jesus address his remarks to "the disciples" (20:45), thereby bringing his themes of reversal and antimaterialism into closer association and with greater impact for his contemporary community.

Balance

Through balanced use, especially of doublets and triads, Luke achieves much of the "orderly" arrangement he assured his patron (1:3) and at the same time suggests what from his viewpoint is the correct interpretation especially of traditions which are obscure or have been subject to misunderstanding. Of related order are numerous other clarifications he gives to items in his narrative. Such an approach permits him—witness the Benedictus—to incorporate traditional positions which, despite their obsolescence, are still of interest to members of the Christian community but in need of interpretive correction or modification. Thus the nationalistic cast of thought in 1:68–71 gives way via 1:72–74 to Luke's numerous emphases and themes that surface in 1:75–79.

From the juxtaposition of two parables in 6:39–42, it is clear that vv. 39–40 present moral critics and their victims under the masks of teacher and pupil. If left as free-floating sayings, the doublet in vv. 43–44 would be obscure. In Luke's narrative they receive a literary home, and having found interpretation in the light of what precedes are themselves endowed with hermeneutical function. Moreover, with the help of the climactic interpretive saying in v. 45 these verses point up the contrast between a spirit of forgiveness and a censorious one.

Luke finds Mark's conjunction of the parable of the sower and its meaning made to order (Luke 8:4–8 and 11–15 = Mark 4:3–8 and 14–20) but isolates the section from Mark's other parables so as to put into sharper focus a favorite theme, "hearing and keeping the word of God."

In 12:1, the phrase "which is hypocrisy" interprets the term "leaven." Facing squarely the tradition of sayings relating to denial of Jesus, which are found as a doublet in Q (Luke 12:8–9 = Matt. 10:32–33), Luke grants the seriousness of the crime of defection, but in 12:10 explains that forgiveness is available even for such offense—he had to admit that Peter was guilty of the crime (22:34, 57); but Jesus prayed for him so that his faith would not "give out" (v. 32). Only refusal to repent, that is, rejection of the Holy Spirit, as displayed in the critique at Acts 28:26–27, finds no forgiveness (Luke 12:10); in brief, those who *will* not see *shall* not see at all.

The doublet in Luke 13:18–21 parallels Matt. 13:31–33 and, in part, Mark 4:30–32, but by placing the two parables in the context of the crippled woman's recovery Luke removes them from the arena of sectarian misunderstanding or arbitrary conjecture. The first of the two parables, suggests Luke, refers to God's outreach to people of whom the crippled woman is representative. Ultimately, as the second parable confirms, God's kingdom will be all-pervasive.

Interpretation of apocalyptic tradition is Luke's forte, and 17:11—18:30 is a representative exhibit of extensive rhetorical clarification on his part. Through the story of the ten lepers he focuses attention on the presence of the kingdom in the benefaction bestowed on the lepers, with emphasis on grateful response to God for Jesus, the chief instrument of divine beneficence. Such response constitutes saving faith. This reference to salvation (v. 19) sets the stage for expanded definition of the kingdom as a two-stage affair. The Pharisees are told that it is "among" them (v. 21). In the succeeding recital, involving Jesus and the disciples (vv. 22–37), no mention is made of the kingdom; instead the focus is on the future day or days of the Son of humanity. Thereby traditional apocalyptic is subsumed under the idea of kingdom rather than made identical with it, and the appearance of Jesus as Son of humanity at the end of the end time is maintained in continuity with his contemporary activity.

But what about the hopes of Jesus' followers for deliverance? Of what relevance is futuristic apocalyptic hope for them? This question receives answer in 18:1–8. God will avenge the elect "speedily" (vv. 7–8). Evidently Luke shares the expectation of many Christians of all ages that history will not go on forever and that God must surely act soon in behalf of the people. But Luke places prime emphasis on the individual's relationship to God rather than on satisfaction of apocalyptic curiosity. Therefore he includes the climactic question: "But, when the Son of humanity comes, will he find faith on the earth?" This question forges a rhetorical link with the story of the ten lepers and prepares the auditor for the point of 18:9–14. The publican, not the Pharisee, went home justified, for the publican acknowledged God as the Supreme Benefactor, who delights in mercy and forgiveness. That is faith, and of the order expressed by the Samaritan (17:15–19). The story ends appropriately with the motif established by the Magnificat: the lofty are brought low and the lowly are exalted (18:14). What is said of the publican and of the Pharisee applies with variation to all who await the end of the end time, and 18:15–17 endorse the conclusion.

In the capitalist's question (18:18) the kingdom in its final phase is defined as "eternal life." But this rich man is also confronted with a summons to realize the kingdom in its present form, that is, in association with Jesus. By declining participation in the first phase he excludes himself from participation in its second phase. Yet how is the man's experience relevant to the Christian community? The disciples have left everything and followed Jesus, but what about the kingdom? Luke finds Mark's entire account compatible with his own two-phase kingdom motif. With slight alteration of diction in 18:29–30 (= Mark 10:29–30) he retains the point that those who sacrifice in the interest of the kingdom receive more "in this time," and "eternal life" is theirs "in the age to come." Behind the statement of present blessing lies Luke's understanding that decision for Jesus requires "endurance" (8:15), for hostility against his mission will cause disruption in households (12:51–53; cf. 21:16–19). But those who hear the word of God and keep it form a new family (8:21), with a new support system, as described in Acts 2:44–47 and 4:32.

Luke 19:1–10 is a model of what constitutes repentance and explains what is meant by God's search for a sinner (chap. 15). The saying, "those who have will receive, but those who have not will be deprived even of what they have" (19:26) required explanation. Some interpretation had been given at 8:18, but the story of the minas (19:11–24), followed by the protest in v. 25, forestalls misunderstanding.

Jesus' pronouncement of woe on his traitor motivates the disciples' debate as to who among them would perpetrate such a deed (22:23). Luke moves the question to the church's larger sphere of experience and shows through vv. 24–34 that the deed of Judas can find expression in a number of ways, and especially in the church's power struggles and contests for turf. Only Jesus' personal intercession can spare Peter ignoble disaster, and he in turn is to strengthen his colleagues (v. 32); that is, the church's leaders are to guard one another against defection.

Echoes

A further contributing factor to the unity of conception and artistic finish of Luke's work is his lavish use of the device of echo diction. It is true that not every hearer or reader of Luke's book would immediately appreciate all of the echoes, nor even some to the same degree as others, but awareness of this circumstance does not diminish the fact of the literary value of the echo-diction any more than one's ignorance of artistic technique when viewing a painting by Rembrandt would detract from that artist's competence. Appreciation takes place at various levels, and it is the interpreter's task to help maximize that appreciation by disclosing a variety of ports of entry into a specific work. Ultimately, discernment of patterns provides controls against over-subtle interpretation derived from prior and often prejudicial assumptions.

Through the story of Jesus' temptation (4:1–11) Luke sets forth the dimensions of the dramatic conflict he develops in his Gospel. Soon after despising Satan's offer of world power ("all this authority," v. 6), Jesus exercises "authority and power" over "unclean demons" (v. 36). Later he deputizes the Twelve with "power and authority over all the demons" (9:1; cf. 10:1–9). But when Jesus says to his enemies from Jerusalem, "This is your hour and the authority of darkness" (22:53), Luke's auditors know that the climactic phase of the dramatic conflict set in motion at 4:1–11 is about to take place. But it was Jerusalem, not Jesus, that closed the deal with Satan. Acts 26:18 puts the mission of Paul on the same wavelength.

Jesus' reply to John's perplexity at Luke 7:22 amplifies the thematic note expressed at 4:18–19. In Luke 7:11–17, the interpretation of Jesus' fulfillment of the expectation expressed in 1:78–79; and 7:36–50, with its emphasis on forgiveness and peace, suggests to Luke's public one of the ways in which 1:79; 2:29–30; and 4:18 are to be understood.

Luke 8:1–3 bears the marks of the evangelist's hand, but at v. 3 he echoes the observation that he had borrowed from Mark 1:31 for inclusion at 4:39. The echo helps to strengthen understanding of Luke's intention at 4:38—5:11 to associate Simon Peter and other disciples with the mission of Jesus.

Through several catchwords and formulaic phrases Luke alerts auditors to the thematic unity of 8:40—9:27. The phrase "you feed them" echoes 8:55. The words "He ordered them to tell no one about it" (9:21) substantially reproduce 8:56. Jesus apportions at 9:1 the power that was at his disposal according to 8:46. At 9:11 Jesus speaks of the kingdom of God and then heals in an example of his own assignment to the disciples at 9:2. From these data it appears that Luke aims to establish as his main point in the feeding narrative that the apostles and their followers are in continuity with the ministry of Jesus. Such would be the case especially after his death and resurrection, events that are signaled by the broken bread and abundance of surviving fragments, as attested also by the further echo at 22:19.

After exposure to Luke 12:11–12, Luke's public would have no difficulty finding a basis for the frequent references to boldness and freedom of speech in the Book of Acts.

The experience of the shepherds (Luke 2:8–14) finds amplification through the echo at 12:32. Assurances in 1:73–74 and 3:8 resound in such passages as 13:16 and 19:9, which in turn echo one another. On the other hand, Abraham is referred to seven times in 16:19–31, and three times the rich man addresses him in direct contradiction to the warning administered at 3:8.

Zacchaeus's repentance (19:8) provides a model for the understanding of 3:13. Luke 19:38 looks backward to 2:14 (but with significant modification of the locale for peace), and also anticipates the pathetic pronouncement of 19:42.

According to 20:17 Jesus is the prime example for the truth of 1:52. In the same pericope, "my beloved son" (20:13) echoes 3:22. In its conditional form the temptation recorded in 23:35 echoes 4:1–11, and "Christ of God" is parallel to "Christ of the Lord" at 2:26. It is indeed ironical that the hierarchy rejects this one who has been so signally attested by the Holy Spirit.

As indicated above, Luke's feeding narrative (9:10–17) is echoed in the eucharistic setting of passion week. The resurrection motif in the earlier narrative is further brought to light by the pains Luke takes to emphasize on the one hand the "waning" of the third day (24:21 and 29; cf. 9:12) and on the other, Jesus' blessing, breaking, and distribution of the bread (24:30; cf. 9:16 and 22:19). The ransom of Israel (24:21) echoes 2:38, but now the auditor hears more.

From the abundant evidence of Luke's predilection for flashback effect it is probable that the "two men" of 24:4 echo 9:30. Having once identified them with the clarification, "who were Moses and Elijah," it was superfluous to repeat the phrase at 24:4.

Quite appropriately Luke concludes his Gospel (24:47) with a reminder of the theme announced at Nazareth (4:18). Forgiveness is God's supreme benefaction (cf. Acts 2:38–39).

Luke's intentions in the arousal of such echoes are further confirmed by associated phenomena in Acts. The Christian community's conception by the Holy Spirit (Acts 1:8) echoes Mary's experience (Luke 1:35), thus confirming the unity of Jesus' and the Christian's mission through the Holy Spirit, who links the action of both with Isaiah's anticipation of the latter-day Servant.

Anticipation

The line between that of rhetorical echo or flashback and of anticipation is a fine one, for writers themselves are interested in lending unity to their work, and what is echo to readers is in many instances fulfillment of what writers had conceived as anticipation of the echo. But there are cases in which authors can presume their public's participation in the literary anticipation, either by virtue of common knowledge of the main lines of the plot, or by sympathetic narrowing of the attention span between anticipation and fulfillment. Examples of the first would, among others, include Luke 2:41–52; 3:16; 4:13; 9:16; 24:34–35; 9:52–56; and 20:9–18, 19–26.

The emphasis in Luke 2:41–52 on Jesus' sonship, together with the geographical focus on Jerusalem and the three-day search, would in all probability suggest to some of Luke's public the denouement in passion week. That the anticipation is also part of the author's literary design is confirmed by the fact that chapters 1 and 2 are especially replete with fundamental data for the understanding of subsequent thematic developments.

Some form of the tradition of the outpouring of the Holy Spirit at Pentecost would be familiar to Luke's public, who would have no difficulty in anticipating at 3:16 a narration of the birthday of the new congregation (Acts 2), especially in view of Luke's promise to write about "what has found fulfillment among us" (Luke 1:1).

At 4:13 Luke could rely on the hearer's sense of tension extending from the desert of temptation to the events of passion week. Especially 22:3, 53 would confirm the expectation. After being exposed to 9:16, some receptors would merely sense in the solemnity of Jesus' gesture a signal of things to come, whereas others would "hear" in the pericope of the feeding of the five thousand the tradition of the last supper (22:19), and all the more audible would be the echoes in 24:30 and Acts 2:46.

Since mission to Samaria was part of the Christians' previous history, Luke's public would be sympathetic to Jesus' rebuke of the disciples in Luke 9:51–56 and they would appreciate the stress on Samaria at Acts 1:8 and subsequent recitals.

Luke knew that his record of Jesus' journey to Jerusalem might strain literary and historical sensitivities. His inclusion of the saying in Luke 13:35 therefore contributes to the dramatic tension and reminds his public that the goal is more than a geographical locale. The hostility and charges expressed in 23:1–3 would probably satisfy anyone who already had exposure to 20:9–18 and 19:26.

Double Sense

A further device employed by Luke to invite depth perception of the plot structure is the use of a term in more than one sense. Part of the auditors' pleasure derives from the expansion of their understanding as the plot unfolds. It is not therefore necessary that they grasp all meanings that the more sophisticated among them might immediately decode.

After the majestic titles accorded Jesus in the pericopes that preceded Luke's recital about the twelve-year-old Jesus, his identification of Jesus as the "boy" (2:43) would not only denote Jesus as child (*pais*) but also connote his role as the Servant (*pais*), who ultimately fulfills Israel's assigned function (see 1:54; cf. Isaiah 41 and 42 and the echoes in Acts 3:13, 26; 4:27, 30).

Given the citation in 4:18–19, the "poor" of 6:20 denote recipients of the promises described, for example, in Isa. 61:1. The term would of course also connote those who, like the widows of Luke 20:47, would suffer oppression in their economically disadvantaged position.

The verb *diatassō* ("he directed") in 8:55 denotes the giving of an order, but connotes authority, such as is commonly expressed in imperial decrees. Some auditors would probably attribute to Luke a ready wit for his use of a verb that was also used as a technical term for testamentary decrees. The meaning of the story is in the conflict of life and death. One might translate: "and it was Jesus' will that she be given something to eat."

At 9:31 it is proper to preserve the double edge of the word *exodus* ("departure"). When Jesus says at 13:32, "on the third day I will be at my goal," Luke's public could be expected to hear the undertones of 12:50.

In the light of 4:18–19, Jesus does more than "send off" a healed man; he "released" him (14:4), even as he had taken a demoniac out of his bonds (see 8:29). This theme of prisoners' release is a favorite of Luke's. In the passion story religious officials ask for the release of the wrong man (23:18). To highlight the contrast between Saul the Inquisitor and Paul the Servant, Luke emphasizes that the apostle to the Gentiles first spent his time in contradicting God's objectives by imprisoning the victims of his misdirected zeal (Acts 8:3; 9:2, 14, 21; 22:4–5; 26:10, an echo of Luke 3:20). Luke 21:24, which seems to contradict 4:18–19, is to be understood in the light of 19:42–44; one of Luke's dramatic devices is to show how glowing hopes, expressed in nationalistic tradition, were aborted by the blindness of Jerusalem's leadership.

In Luke 20:36 the term "sons of God" denotes pious human beings, but the term is often used to denote angels; given the context, Luke here engages in a deft bit of word play. In the face of Jesus' repartee, the Sadducees, who deny both the existence of angels and the resurrection (Acts 23:8), are faced with affirmation of both.

According to Luke 22:56 Peter faces the "light (of the fire)," but Luke's public knows that Peter is really in the presence of Jesus, who was once identified by Simeon as a "light for revelation to the Gentiles" (2:32) and who now turns to "look" (22:61) at his cowardly disciple. The double sense functions, therefore, as a rhetorical device to call attention to the presence of Jesus, thus motivating the dramatic climax at v. 61. And with superb economy it enunciates the grossness of Peter's act.

At Acts 16:29 the guard "asked for a light," and Luke's auditor knows well the source! When the jailer goes on to address Paul and Silas as "Lords (Sirs)," the apostles quickly correct him, "Believe in the one Lord Jesus." So also, with slight change of phrase, had James and John spoken at Pentecost (3:12).

Satire and Irony

A few examples of satire and irony conclude this survey of rhetorical devices in Luke's work. At Luke 12:14 Jesus does indeed disclaim the role of judge in a court of petty claims, but Luke's public does not first have to read Acts 10:42 to give an appropriate reply to Jesus' question. The "man out of the crowd" (Luke 12:13) hears more than he bargained for. Ironically, his query exposes him to an encounter with Yahweh, whose indictments of covetousness are common knowledge through Moses and now endorsed through Jesus.

Profound pathos permeates the grim resolution expressed in 13:33 and the description of Jerusalem's claim to fame (v. 34; cf. Acts 3:13–15). The dramatic effect of the irony in 22:37–38 has already been noted. One of the most elegant blends of satire and irony ever recorded appears at Luke 24:18. Kings who have undertaken rash campaigns are sketched with brisk economy (14:30). And what Luke has to say about the psychology of crowds has probably never found a pithier challenge than the verdict in Acts 19:32: "Most of the people did not know why they were there" (cf. the fickleness described in Luke 7:24–27). This is satire in the style of Horace, criticism without mordacity. It derives from the same wells of compassion as the puncturing of society's pitiful scrambling for prestige (14:30).

And somewhere in this twilight of redemptive humor there gleams the pronouncement at Luke 23:43, in which Jesus, alleged criminal, assumes the role of a benefactor and in an executive capacity decrees amnesty for the repentant malefactor.

PART 2

"LIGHT TO THE GENTILES"

CHAPTER THREE

EXCEPTIONAL MERIT AND BENEFICENCE

In the Greco-Roman world special attention was paid to people who were distinguished for exceptional merit. Homer's epics celebrated Achilles, Hector, and other mighty warriors as such superstars. In the course of centuries there developed a democratization of excellence. A variety of public officials, athletes, physicians, priests, officers of private associations, and others received recognition and awards for special service to their city or nation. But rulers retained the firmest grip on the people's adulation, often expressed in fulsome expressions of thanks for their benefactions.

Since numerous terms were used to describe such philanthropists, it is important to note that the English word "benefactor" as used in this book has no single Greek expression as referent, but takes account of a Greco-Roman cultural reality that covered a broad range of social phenomena and included human beings and deities in its scope. The manner in which Luke encodes this feature is one of the many interesting facets of his work. But at all times one must keep in mind that the concept of a person of exceptional merit is the primary idea, and that beneficence happens to be the principal point of interest for Greco-Roman consideration of anyone's merit.

According to Dio Chrysostom, a ruler is most powerful and magnificently royal when he tends to the needs of his subjects. Such expression of concern finds frequent utterance in the synonyms *sōzō* and *euergeteō* ("save" and "render benefaction"). The term *sōtēr* (savior) was an official title among the Ptolemies and the Seleucids. This noun was also applied, usually unofficially, in Luke's time to Roman emperors and public benefactors of lesser prestige, and is used here and there in conjunction with the noun *euergetēs* or its cognates.

Hellenistic Benefactors

No ancient secular document serves so well to outline the kind of thought-world in which Luke moved with his conceptions of Jesus as does the famous inscription of Priene, in the province of Asia, celebrating the birthday of Caesar Augustus. It is dated 9 B.C. Our translation indicates in brackets the words that are especially significant for appreciation of Luke's proclamation:

CAESAR AUGUSTUS

Letter of the Proconsul in Praise of
Caesar on his Birthday

[Paulus Fabius Maximus to the Asian League, greeting. . . .] It is subject to question whether the birthday of our most divine Caesar spells more of joy or blessing, this being a date that we could probably without fear of contradiction equate with the beginning of all things, if not in terms of nature, certainly in terms of utility, seeing that he restored stability, when everything was collapsing and falling into disarray, and gave a new look to the entire world that would have been most happy to accept its own ruin had not the good and common fortune of all been born: CAESAR.

Therefore people might justly assume that his birthday spells the beginning of life and real living and marks the end and boundary of any regret that they had themselves been born. . . . And whereas on the one hand it is difficult to render thanks in proportion to the many benefits [euergetēmata] he has conferred— unless, of course, we pondered carefully how we might in some way requite them one by one; and whereas on the other hand it may be presumed that people will more readily celebrate as a birthday a day that is already observed in common by all, especially if it offers them a measure of leisure because it coincides with the (local) inaugural observance, it is my judgment that the one and the same day observed by all the citizens as New Year's Day be celebrated as the birthday of Most Divine Caesar, and on that day, September 23, all elected officials shall assume office, with the prospect that through association with observances connected with the existing celebration, the birthday observance might attract all the more esteem and prove to be even more widely known and thereby confer no small benefit on the province. Therefore it would behoove the Asian League to pass a resolution that puts into writing all his aretai [evidences of superior excellence], so that our recognition of what redounds to the honor of Augustus might abide for all time. And I shall order the decree to be inscribed in (Greek and Latin) on a stele and set up in the temple.

The Decree of the Popular Assembly
of the Asian League

Decree of the Greek Assembly in the province of Asia, on motion of the High Priest Apollonios, son of Menophilos, of Aizonoi: WHEREAS Providence that orders all our affairs has in her display of concern and generosity in our behalf adorned our lives with the highest good: Augustus, whom she has unusually endowed for the benefit [euergesia] of humanity, and has in her beneficence granted us and those who will come after us [a Savior] who has made war to cease and who shall put everything [in peaceful] order; and whereas Caesar, [when he was manifest], transcended the expectations of [all who had anticipated the good news], not only by surpassing the benefits conferred by his predecessors but by leaving no expectation [elpis] of surpassing him to those who will come after him, with the result that the birth date of our God signalled the beginning of Good News [euaggelia, in connection with celebrations] for the world because of him; (and whereas) proconsul Paulus Fabius Maximus, benefactor [euergeteō] of the province, who had been dispatched for its security [sōtēria] by (Caesar's) authority and decision, besides all the other benefits that he had already conferred on the province, so many in fact that no one would be able to calculate them, has contributed yet one more, and so has discovered a way to honor Augustus that was hitherto unknown among the Greeks, namely to reckon time from the date of his nativity; therefore . . . be it decreed that the New Year begin for all the cities on September 23, which is the birthday of Augustus. . . .[1]

NERO

Finally, a notorious successor from Luke's own lifetime receives this accolade:

To Nero Claudius Caesar Augustus Germanicus Emperor, Savior [sōtēr] and Benefactor [euergetēs] of the world. . . .[2]

As Acts 15 attests, Luke knows well the language of decrees, and he even begins his two-volume work with the familiar form: "Inasmuch as . . . therefore I resolved . . ." (Luke 1:1–4). Some of his Greco-Roman public would catch a double sense and note that what followed in his work contained the details of the proclamation of JESUS THE GREAT, BENEFACTOR OF HUMANITY. God, SŌTĒR (Savior, 1:47), gives Jesus to the world as climactic benefaction.

Jesus—Benefactor of All Benefactors

To express the function of Jesus as Beneficent Savior, Luke lays stress on the name Jesus. As Semitic equivalent of sōtēr, it would speak to Hellenistic Jew and non-Jew alike and could also arouse association with a wealth of OT tradition.

Since the names Jesus and Joshua are alternate ways of transliterating one and the same Greek word, Luke's Jewishly oriented public would not have the same problem experienced by modern readers of the Bible. They would immediately recognize in the Nazarene's name an echo of the Jesus who led Israel into the promised land (rendered "Joshua" in translation of the OT, but in the King James Version of Acts 8:45 and Hebrews 4:8, "Jesus"). This OT Jesus enjoyed Moses' reputation for close relationships to Yahweh (Josh. 3:7) and accomplished what Moses failed to accomplish—the entry into Canaan. He fulfilled all the orders given to Moses and gave peace to the land (Josh. 3:7; cf. 21:45).

The intimate relation of the Father and the Son and their common objective, to bestow salvation, are carefully enunciated in the first two chapters of Luke's Gospel. This section is indelibly marked by Luke's editorial pen, and within it there appear five instances (1:47, 69, 71, 77; 2:11, 30) out of Luke's total usage (17×) of the terms *sōtēr* and *sōtēria*. That Luke finds these terms attractive because of their prevalence in Greek versions of the Jewish Scriptures is beyond dispute, but he can count on Greco-Roman auditors who may have no contact with those writings to grasp the significance of Jesus' arrival on the scene.

They, as well as Hellenized Jews, would know that these terms were standard in bureaucratic and sacral documents relating to benefactors—not to speak of literary and private writings—and their use in association with the person and work of Jesus would provide an appropriate hermeneutical medium. Together with other features in Luke's first two chapters, these terms help inform Luke's auditors that his two-volume account is about God's action in connection with Jesus Christ, Great Benefactor.

Word and Deed

Linkage of deeds and words in connection with depiction of human as well as divine excellence is, of course, common in the Old Testament, but the formulation "word and deed" is especially typical of accolades to Greek or Roman benefactors and finds expression in such formulae as "(distinguished) for word and deed" and "saying and doing what is good."[3]

Accompanying a long tradition of respect for responsible civic action is the natural desire of Hellenic communities to maintain politicians at peak performance. In a decree dated 211–210, Athenians awarded honors for a praetor who had rendered distinguished service, "neither excusing himself from any personal hardship or danger, but in word and deed doing everything advantageous to the country."[4] An oath of the Paphlagonians of Galatia, incised about 3 B.C., inverts the usual procedure and promises allegiance to the royal family "in word (*logos*) and deed (*ergon*) and mind (*gnōmē*)."[5]

In literary writings the juxtaposition finds expression as early as Homer, in Phoenix's description of Achilles as "an orator and a man of action" (*Iliad* 9.443). It is used with variations by such historians as Thoukydides and Polybios. Apart from the passages in Luke that are discussed below, related formulations appear in Rom. 15:18; 2 Cor. 10:11; Col. 3:17; 2 Thess. 2:17; 1 John 3:18.

The laudatory word-deed formulation emphasizes that the person so described performs in keeping with his rhetoric. Negative variations can be devastating. A master of the latter was the Greek orator Demosthenes, in his attack on Aischines in *On the Crown*. Similarly, Epiktetos says that a person of exceptional merit ought to be distinguished for deeds and not merely words (3.24.110). And the historian Eunapios (A.D. 4–5) adapted the formulation in a satirical evaluation of a king named Prohairesios: "Rome ruled one who reigned in words." Luke's own variation of the satire appears in 22:24–26: "Those who have authority over them (the nations) like to have themselves called benefactors" (*euergetai*). The middle voice of the present tense of the

Greek verb calls attention to the self-interest of these bureaucrats. The admonition in 22:26, "You shall not be so," takes into account the entire statement, not merely, as some commentators have erroneously assumed, the one word (*euergetai*). The disciples' stance is to be that of Jesus'—one of service, unmotivated by lust for power. This is the road of true beneficence. That Luke intended the passage to be so understood is clear from the fact that at Acts 4:9–12 Jesus is declared in effect to be a benefactor, and at 10:38 he is explicitly so termed: "Benefactor (*euergetōn*) that he was, he went about healing all who were being tyrannized by the Devil."[6]

As is apparent from his own review of his first volume, Luke considers what Jesus "began to do and to teach" (Acts 1:1; cf. 10:38) the substance of the Great Benefactor's mission, and with this the church is forthwith identified. Appropriately therefore, Luke reserves the classic description of a Hellenistic Benefactor for some dialogue that takes place *after* Jesus' resurrection: "He was a prophet powerful in action as well as word," says Cleopas (Luke 24:19). "And," he plaintively concludes, "we were confident that he would rescue Israel. But after everything that's happened in Jerusalem, and now it being far into the third day—well, we just don't know" (v. 21). Many of Luke's auditors, being in on the plot, enjoy the suspenseful scene for they know that Jesus' resurrection is the climactic deed that cashes their Savior's verbal promissory note issued in predictions of his passion and resurrection (9:22; 18:33). After Jesus, only one other person qualifies for the accolade. In Acts 7:22 Luke has Stephen repeat almost verbatim about Moses (terms reversed, and plural instead of singular) the formula uttered by Cleopas, "and he was powerful in his words and deeds." Both Jesus and Moses are benefactors par excellence, but Jesus effects an "exodus" (see Luke 9:31) that supersedes Moses' accomplishment.[7]

Jesus as Healer

In keeping with the main verdict, Luke throughout his Gospel presents Jesus as powerful orator (prophet) and performer of mighty deeds. Already at the age of twelve he astounds his elders (2:47). So firmly does Jesus weld action to word that he adopts the OT as his scenario and consumes his life in the necessity of fulfilling his Father's purpose. Thus, 2:49 after numerous echoes finds further eloquent expression in 24:44.

About two decades after his visit to Jerusalem, he identifies himself at Nazareth with Isaiah's "Servant" (4:18), the Jewish counterpart of the Hellenistic superstar.[8] The people of Nazareth cannot believe their ears (4:22), and it is evident from Jesus' words in v. 23 that they are looking for the second component, confirmatory action. Luke is quick to provide it, and his editing of Mark's healing narratives, together with his choice of other accounts and the Greco-Roman themes and formulations associated with them, confirm his interest in Greco-Roman systems of beneficence as models for understanding the significance of Jesus.

At 4:36, Luke clarifies Mark 1:27 by altering "What is this?" to "What is this word?" (Luke 4:36). Jesus' rhetoric reduces an unclean spirit into innocuous submission. In place of Mark's statement (1:31) of personal contact with Simon Peter's mother-in-law, Luke declares (4:39) that Jesus rebuked her fever, with immediate results.[9] To focus further attention on the power of Jesus' word, Luke alters Mark's "they say" to "they asked."

Luke's recital of healings at Capernaum provides the component that appeared to be missing at Nazareth (Luke 4:23), and a second series of recitals in 5:1—6:11 further verifies Luke's evident intention to interpret Jesus in terms of a person of distinguished merit.

At 4:44 Luke picks up Mark's observation that Jesus was "preaching" and begins a series of narratives that climaxes with Jesus' words to the envoys of John the Baptist (7:22-23). Between these two passages are recitals that interpret Jesus as a person of extraordinary merit because of a mastery in words that is reinforced by exceptional deeds.

In his introduction to the story of the abundant catch of fish (5:1-11), a recital not found in Mark or Matthew, Luke refers twice to the oratorical power of Jesus (vv. 1, 3). Upon the command of Jesus (v. 4), Simon and his crew head for the deep, and their obedience is rewarded by a beneficence that astounds them all (v. 8).

The power of Jesus' word to heal a leper (5:12-16) generates further spread of "the story about Jesus" (v. 15). Luke's revision here eliminates Mark's reference to the healed leper as a proclaimer (cf. Mark 1:45) and sets the stage for his implicit conjunction of word ("many crowds heard") and deed ("many were healed") in v. 15.

To stress the functional aspect of the word-deed theme in 5:17-26, Luke first shifts Mark's "he was speaking the word to them" (2:2) to the beginning of v. 17, but in revised form: "he was teaching." This revision discourages dissipation of attention that is to be preserved for the moment when the power of Jesus' word comes to dramatic expression (v. 24). In the vacated position Luke introduces a new statement, "the Lord's healing power was with Jesus," and thus anticipates the question about power or ability raised at v. 21.

After a section (5:27—6:5) in which Jesus' pandemic, universal outreach and liberating message are reviewed by his opposition, Luke further reinforces his interpretation of Jesus as a superstar by revisions he makes (6:6-11) in Mark's (3:1-6) story about a man with a withered hand. As at 5:17, Luke adds in the very first verse (6:6) that Jesus was teaching. To sharpen a contrast between benefactor and malefactor, Luke alters Mark's two-word expression (to "do good," *agathon poiēsai*) to a single term (to "benefit," *agathopoiēsai*). So as not to vitiate the purity of Jesus' beneficence, Luke deletes Mark's reference (3:5) to Jesus' feelings about the opposition, thereby permitting the command of Jesus to stand in dramatic isolation with the restoration of the man's hand. In place of Mark's reference (3:6) to a death-plot by Pharisees and Herodians, Luke offers a more moderate version of the opposition's hostility. His use of the term *anoia* (rage) would suggest to Luke's auditors the cognate term *eunoia*, which is frequently used in Greco-Roman description of persons of exceptional merit. The contrary attitude of the opposition thus highlights the beneficent approach of Jesus that pervades Luke's entire account and at the same time suggests the necessity of a replacement for Israel's leadership, a need that is met in the selection of the Twelve (vv. 12–16).

To focus attention on the significance of the Sermon on the Plain as the climactic expression of Jesus' power in word, Luke not only shifts Mark 3:7–12 to a position after his own recital of the appointment of the Twelve, but revises Mark's statement (3:8) about the reputation that Jesus enjoyed so as to incorporate the word-deed concept. They came to hear Jesus, who speaks with benedictions, and to be healed of their diseases (Luke 6:17). In the actual Sermon on the Plain Jesus speaks with the authority of an emperor and climaxes his presentation with an ultimate claim on the lives and consciences of the hearers, who are themselves in turn invited to participate as co-benefactors, who match their confessional words with affirmative action (Luke 6:46–49). Their generosity (vv. 27–38) is to be rooted in the character of God as Supreme Benefactor (v. 35).

The stories recited in 7:1–22 confirm the authority of the words recited on the plain, and they bring Luke's auditors full circle to the inaugural message pronounced at 4:18–19.

In the heavily edited story of the centurion (7:1–9), much of the point hinges on the dramatic encounter of two benefactors, the soldier who built a synagogue (v. 5), and Jesus, whose authoritative word accomplishes what invincible Roman power can only courteously request. Alert auditors would have noted the connection with the point made in 4:25–29. Jesus' words will outlast the universe (21:33) and the celestial palace door will slam shut against those who are ashamed of their Benefactor's words (13:25–30; 9:26).

The ultimate test of verbal power is encounter with death. Luke's Superstar has only to say the one word "Rise!" and death is conquered. Elegantly interpolated between the personal address and this command is the phrase, "I say to you" (= "my word to you is"). The response of the people is an affirmation of what Luke called "the things fulfilled among us" (1:1). God's prophetic word has been realized in powerful action, and this declared fact spreads far and wide in Israel's land (7:17).

It was not lost on Luke's auditors that the widow of Nain joined a widow of earlier times in receipt of a singular benefit (cf. 4:25–26), and they are now prepared for the account about John the Baptist's problem, which is essentially that of the people in Nazareth (4:23). One can assume that Luke would expect his auditors to amplify what is implicit in the statement about John's perplexity, "Where is the performance, such as deliverance of the captives that was pronounced in the inaugural address?" (4:18). The evident allusion to 4:18–19 in 7:22 suggests the validity of this inference. Jesus' reply to John incorporates the word-deed pair. The envoys are to report the deeds they have "seen" and the words they have "heard" (v. 22). Specific items are included in the second part of v. 22, with climactic stress on the word of Jesus ("the poor are receiving [God's] proclamation").

Among the benefactions ascribed to Isis is mastery over the sea.[10] Similarly Jesus makes Lake Genesseret safe for travel by rebuking its raging waters (Luke 8:25).

In a striking departure from Mark's reference (6:30) to the disciples' report of "what they had done and of what they had taught," Luke (9:10) records only that they recited "what they had done." The revision is consistent with Luke's implicit critique of a one-sided report that was given by the Seventy (10:17).

Outreach in Healing

Numerous Hellenic inscriptions published in celebration of healings conferred by physicians incorporate the theme of an honorand's interest in the well-being of all who were in need of services, including those who were outside the physician's geographic locality. Frequently such pandemic or general help was extended without hope of recompense.[11]

Luke's general fondness for the adjective "all" is consonant with his perception of the universal outreach of God in Jesus. And since a reputation for pandemic approach was highly prized by benefactors, Luke includes in connection with his appraisal of Jesus as benefactor at Acts 10:38 that he cured "all" who were oppressed by the devil. In this passage Luke himself declares that his record of Jesus' healings was designed to project Jesus as a benefactor, and his editing of Mark's accounts reveals the rationale for his reference to "all" in the Acts passage. Mindful of the interests of his Greco-Roman auditors, and in keeping with the thematic note in Luke 2:10 (cf. 2:31, 38) of God's pandemic outreach, Luke modifies several of Mark's passages so as to highlight the universal outreach in the New Age.

Mark 1:32–34 refers to an undefined number of people who were bringing "all the sick and the possessed" to Jesus, but the conclusion states that he healed "many." In his edition of the account, Luke states that "all who had sick people among them" (4:40) brought their patients to Jesus. His rendering suggests not only a large number of invalids but implies that no one was considered ineligible to bring a sick person to Jesus. Luke emphatically states in the conclusion to this recital that Jesus healed them all by putting his hands "on each one of them" (v. 40). At 6:19, in place of Mark's "he healed many"

(3:10), Luke reads, "and he was healing all of them." Luke registers the importance of his own editorial change by amplifying an echo of this passage in Acts 5:16: "all were being healed."

To provide a broad geographical base for the healing activity of the Twelve, Luke (9:6) reads in place of Mark's reference (6:13) to their healing of "many" that they cured people "everywhere." The alteration is similar to his broadening of the range of John's activity at 3:3 (cf. Mark 1:4).

Response to Healings

Luke's attention to formulation of response in healing narratives is a further indicator of his awareness of the emphasis placed in Greco-Roman society on the services of benefactors.

An inscription, from about the middle of the second century, in praise of God Asklepios, displays variations of the doxology:

> In those very days (our God Asklepios) revealed to a certain blind man named Gaius to come to the base (of the statue) and worship, then to go from the right to the left and to place his five fingers on the base and to lift up his hand and hold it to his eyes; and his sight was clear, as the crowd stood by and rejoiced with him because life-giving powers showed themselves in the presence of our Augustus Antoninus.
>
> God revealed to Lucius, afflicted with pleurisy, and given up by everyone, to come and take ashes from the altar to the Three Gods, and mix them up well with wine and to apply the mixture in the afflicted area. And he was healed and gave thanks publicly to God, and the people rejoiced with him.[12]

Luke's account of the ten lepers (17:12-19) is unique in the gospel tradition and appears to have been chosen specifically to make an impact on Greco-Roman auditors. Apart from presenting God as the Supreme Benefactor and Jesus as the instrument for divine beneficence, the story focuses on appropriate response to such beneficence. Within the context of Luke's total work, the attitude of the nine ungrateful lepers is typical of the negative response made especially by Israel's leaders to the work and message of Jesus and the apostles. Other narratives peculiar to Luke that feature doxologies include 7:11-17 and 13:10-17.

Further indications of Luke's interest in this specific aspect of a Greco-Roman cultural pattern are two revisions of Mark's recitals of Jesus' healing activity. At 5:25-26 (cf. Mark 2:12) he calls attention to the fact that the healed man, as well as the crowd, glorified God. In the story of the blind man healed at Jericho (Luke 18:35-43; cf. Mark 10:46-52) Luke observes that he glorified God and that "all the people gave praise to God."

Especially significant is the manner in which Luke leaves a Greco-Roman impress near the beginning and the end of his story of Jesus' climactic performance at Jerusalem. At 19:37 (cf. Mark 11:9) Luke notes that the multitude of disciples were praising God for all the demonstrations of power that they had observed. Then, at 23:47, Luke adds to Mark's (15:39) version of the centurion's attitude that he "glorified God" in the face of what he had seen. The entire story of Jesus' suffering is thus endowed with additional meaning for Greco-Roman auditors. Jesus goes to his death in a most glorious display of divine beneficence and a Roman public official acknowledges this—he praised God (*edoxadzen ton theon;* cf. Luke 4:15; 8:39; 17:18).

Luke's accounts in Acts concerning the miraculous confirm the preceding line of interpretation. Through the healing of the lame man, the God of Israel's most illustrious ancestors has "glorified" Jesus (Acts 3:13). The benefit (*euergesia*, 4:9) bestowed on the lame man does not derive from Peter and John but from Jesus. And Luke terminates this parade piece with the observation that "all the people glorified God (*edoxadzon ton theon*) over what had taken place" (4:21).

The story of Peter's encounter with Cornelius (10:1—11:18) is similarly recited at length and with fullness of detail. As in the earlier account, the Greco-Roman benefactor model is used in Peter's interpretive speech, thus providing Luke an opportunity to expand on his interpretation of Jesus as a person of extraordinary merit (10:38). In accordance with the mandate recited in Luke 24:48, the disciples attest his performance (Acts 10:39). As in the story of the healing of the lame man, the Christians in Jerusalem respond to God's beneficence in conferring the Holy Spirit on Cornelius and his family, thereby confirming that the Gentiles have a share in the "life" (11:18) of the New Age. Gentiles in turn glorify God for the message that includes them as participants in eternal life (13:48). At 21:20 Paul's audience glorifies God after hearing his report about what God had done among the Gentiles through his ministry.[13]

With word-deed as model, Luke is able to interpret Jesus in terms of the Roman-Hellenistic Benefactor. But Luke observed that, unlike politicians whose deeds can never rise to the level of their rhetoric, or whose performance may not be in conformity with expressed principle, Jesus brought deed and word to such a level of coincidence and concurrence that he is unique in the history of politics. A historian-theologian of rare political acumen, Luke grasped to an extraordinary degree the inherent drama of Jesus' identification with the reign of God in the face of apparently insuperable odds. Jesus is indeed the Superstar of superstars. But superstar status, especially for heads of state, means acceptance of hazard and being cast in the role of endangered benefactor.

The Endangered Benefactor

Original in his politics, Jesus achieved what many a politician likes to affirm of himself. He was his own man. But he won his identity by identifying himself totally with his Father's purpose. Those who lose their life save it was an axiom he never questioned (9:24). At the very beginning of his recital of Jesus' public ministry Luke therefore carefully distinguishes Jesus' personal experience in the presence of God from John the Baptist's activity at the Jordan (3:21–22). The Spirit's descent and the genealogy confirm on the one hand the uniqueness of Jesus as Son of God and at the same time his intimate participation in the experience of humanity (3:21–38). With such credentials Jesus confronts his political adversary, the devil (Diabolos). By his arrangement of the temptations, Luke shows how clearly the lines of conflict are drawn from the very start.

These are two very determined antagonists. But it would be a mistake to assume that the devil is irreligious. Luke lets us know that the demonic majesty acknowledges a higher source for his power. The devil's mistake is that he thinks the essence of power is the clever trade, the quid pro quo, the deal. Making himself out as the world's dispenser of benefactions, he says, "Worship me, and all that you see will be yours." Put in politicalese: "Be practical. Religion has its place, but don't be a fanatic. You might as well know it, what counts is power and cash. I've got friends in high places. See, there's Jerusalem and Rome."

Jesus rebuffed the cosmic bribe, and the devil departs to await a more convenient opportunity (4:13). The right moment will come (22:3) when this crusader for God is discredited by his own followers, who will refuse to be taken in any longer by his fantastic dreams and unrealistic proposals for living. What does this carpenter know about life? Such a waste of good political talent! Thus Luke links the beginning and the end in terms of divergent political ideologies, and Jerusalem, traditional seat of Israel's power and potential candidate for apocalyptic supremacy, is the decisive locale.

Crisis Faced by Beneficiaries

Greco-Roman auditors would readily grasp the lines of the main plot. Descriptions of ancient benefactors, especially those engaged in duties of state, frequently include references to the hazards or crises that they undergo on behalf of their people. The technical term for such courageous action in the line of duty is "persistasis," derived from a Greek word, which was one of numerous synonyms used by ancient civic committees in reference to endangered benefactors.

About the year 48 B.C., the people of Dionosypolis, a city near the Black Sea, praised a philanthropist named Akornion, for risking "life and limb in any crisis (*peristasis*) that developed."[14]

Of an otherwise unknown bureaucrat named Menas, it is stated that he "spares no expense in rendering public service nor gives thought to any hazard (*kindynos*) that imperils his own interests when he leaves on embassies in behalf of the city."[15]

The inscription goes on to declare that he "bore (*hypomenō*) his public service out of love for the good (*philagathon*)" (lines 27–28). As is frequently the case in laudatory documents, the term *anēr agathos* in this document here functions as a synonym of *euergetēs*, and is appropriately rendered "benefactor." The document explicitly states that one who rescues others from danger qualifies for recognition as a philanthropist.

Death, the Ultimate Hazard

From the foregoing inscriptions and the many more that could be cited it is evident that the theme of the endangered benefactor is public property in the Hellenistic world and is not the occasional expression of romanticizing philosophers or poets. But it is only natural that a benefactor's endurance of death as the ultimate hazard should have become the subject of poetic and oratorical exposition.

Few tales in antiquity expressed the topic more poignantly than did the story of Alkestis, daughter of Pelias and Anaxibia and wife of Admetos who was doomed to an early death because of impiety. As told by Hyginus, Apollo had agreed that "another could volunteer to die in Admetos's place." When neither his father nor his mother was willing to die for him, Alkestis offered herself. Shortly thereafter Herakles made his appearance and brought her back from the nether regions. Euripides gave the myth its classic treatment in the *Alkestis*, in which Admetos upbraids his aged father Pheres for lacking the courage and the will to die in his behalf.

Also popular was the account about the fidelity of Phintias, a Pythagorean philosopher, to his friend Damon. According to Iamblichos, a Syracusan king named Dionysios related the story. In a manner reminiscent of the testing of Job's integrity by the satan, the probity and loyalty of the two Pythagoreans was put to the test. Phintias was accused of plotting the death of Dionysios. When Dionysios confronted him and pronounced a death sentence, Phintias asked that he be given the remainder of the day to settle his affairs and offered to supply a hostage. Astonished, Dionysios asked whether such a person even existed, one who would risk his own neck in pledge for another. Phintias assured him that there was indeed such a person and forthwith summoned Damon. The latter, again to Dionysios's astonishment, agreed to the arrangement. The Pythagoreans' detractors scoffed and predicted that Damon would be left holding the bag. But just as the sun was about to sink Phintias, prepared to accept his execution, made his appearance. In the face of the opposition's discomfiture, Dionysios embraced the young men and pleaded to be admitted into their friendship pact. His request was denied.[16]

In his essay on friendship, titled *Toxaris* (20), Lucian alludes to the legendary loyalty of Phintias when he has Toxaris addressed in these words:

> What firmer display of goodwill could one make to a friend who has fallen over-
> board into a raging sea at night than to share his death? Let your eyes take in for

a moment the aweful cresting of the waves, the crashing roar of waters, the rolling boiling spume, the darkness, the despair. Then behold the one man, his lungs filling with water, scarcely holding up his head, hands reaching out for his friend; now see the other frantically plunging toward him and swimming with him, fearful lest this Damon should perish first.

This recital is indicative of the power of story to generate awareness of simile, which in turn generates new narrative as a metaphoric entity. It is but a short step to the interpretation of historical events in terms of folk story grammar and figure. Below we shall see how this generative principle is operative in the manner in which various publics perceive Luke's meaning especially in the passion account.

Orators echo the judgment of the poets. In a fragment attributed without justification to the brilliant orator Demades (fl. about 350–319), the pseudonymous author incorporates the topos of the ultimate hazard and uses diction that is commonly associated with a benefactor's performance:

If by my death I am in a position to contribute something to the common welfare (*pros tēn koinēn sōtērian*), I am prepared to die. For the winning of goodwill through one's own death is a noble enterprise, if the sacrifice of death redounds to the interests of the city and not to the rhetorical prestige of my opponents.[17]

Woe to the one who is unwilling to run the risk. With withering scorn Lysias asks his audience why Andokides should receive any consideration: "For the conferment of what benefit (*euergesia*)? Because he incurred danger on account of you many times in behalf of (*hyper*) the city?"[18]

Quite evidently it is taken for granted in the Mediterranean world that acceptance of risks in behalf of others displays nobility, but to pay the ultimate price in service to friends or city is the outstanding mark of *aretē* or superb excellence.

That Luke so views the death of Jesus Christ is apparent from Acts 10:35–43. First Luke has Peter make reference to "word" in conjunction with a depiction of Jesus. Jesus proclaimed "peace" (vv. 35–36), one of the main features of a benefactor's claim to recognition (see below). But performance must accompany utterance if a benefactor is to enjoy credibility. Luke covers this aspect in 10:37–38, in which he explicitly terms Jesus a "benefactor" through use of the verb *euergeteō*. The extraordinary nature of his performance is defined in the words about his powerful healings. The fact that they overpower the devil attests their uniqueness. No Greco-Roman could escape the conclusion—this Jesus of Nazareth is an exceptional person, a man of *aretē*, a benefactor, Superstar of superstars. But at v. 39 Luke goes on to emphasize his superstar performance so as to provide a climactic background for the role of Jesus as an endangered benefactor: "whom you destroyed when you hung him on the timber." Yet through his death Jesus becomes the instrument of further extraordinary beneficence—divine forgiveness (v. 43). These words from Acts 10 are in effect an exposition of Jesus' own self-identification as an endangered benefactor on the night of his betrayal: "This is my body which is given for you" (Luke 22:19). His followers would also learn to be endangered benefactors. Of Paul and Barnabas it was said that they "risked their lives for the sake of our Lord Jesus Christ" (Acts 15:26).

Luke's outreach in Acts 10 to his Greco-Roman public through diction and mode of narration that suggested one of their most common cultural experiences echoes Acts 4:9–10, where Luke connects beneficence and incurred hazard. Beyond question a benefit (*euergesia*) has been conferred. But by whom? Answer: Jesus Christ of Nazareth. This is immediately followed by a declaration about the ultimate price he paid: "whom you crucified." Yet through the very death for which they are guilty they can be saved (vv. 11–12).

The importance of Nazareth in Luke's narrative is not to be underestimated, and Acts 4:9–12 signals the perspective from which Jesus' initial appearance there is to be understood. In the first two chapters of Luke's Gospel, God is described as Savior (1:47) and so is Jesus (2:11). Faced with the child Jesus in his arms, the righteous and devout Simeon declares that then and there he beholds God's salvation (2:30). He follows this identification with a statement about the hazards with which Jesus must cope, at great cost also to his mother (vv. 34–35). The story of the temptation in effect dramatizes Simeon's forecast of Jesus' role as endangered benefactor. And between 4:13 and 22:3 Luke describes Jesus' consolidation of power before his climactic clash with the satan. Dominating this main narrative sequence is the inaugural address and accompanying events at Nazareth (4:16–30).

Luke tells of Jesus reading selected passages that have to do with the mission of the Servant of the Lord (4:18–19). Remarkable is the use of the verb for anointing, which would suggest the title "Christ." Acts 10:38 affirms that Jesus was given his messianic credentials by the Holy Spirit, and these were displayed in powerful, beneficent ways.

Included in Jesus' inaugural address is a list of benefits to be bestowed in the New Age that has dawned with the arrival of God's Anointed One. Jesus' speech at Nazareth was so powerful that it elicited an immediate death sentence. The devil's desert place (4:2) and Nazareth were not really too far apart, but no respectable prophet dies outside Jerusalem (13:33). And so it is that Jesus escapes for the present. But Luke's manner of telling about Jesus' experience at Nazareth helps many in the evangelist's public to place Jesus in the context of their cultural experience of the endangered benefactor. Moreover, Luke's interest in the motif of the endangered benefactor to a large extent accounts for some of the literary difficulties alleged for this narrative.[19]

Indeed, after Nazareth it was clear that Jesus would be politically in debt to no one but his heavenly Parent, but the price would be high. People unaccustomed to his unique politics would find his answers exasperating. What kind of Messiah was this who alienated followers who wanted just a little time to think it over before they walked into the future (Luke 9:59–62)? And how could one who claimed to make others fishers of people work so hard on losing so prominent a catch as the man who asked how he might inherit eternal life (18:18)? After all, he did show more sense than the man who wanted help in getting a fair split on an inheritance (12:13). What future is in store for a person who lacks diplomatic civility to such degree?

Luke injects other forecasts. Herod Antipas is viewed as an anti-benefactor figure in Luke 3:19. Greco-Roman publics were accustomed to having monuments record the praises of officials "for all the good things that they had done." Contrary to expectation, Luke says of Herod that John rebuked him "for all the wicked things that he had done." John's apprehension under Antipas serves as a proleptic image of the hazards that await Jesus, and sharpness is lent to it at 13:31–35. In this latter passage we have a twofold hint of the death of Jesus (vv. 31, 33). After each of these ominous forebodings Luke includes a reference to the beneficence of Jesus. Verse 32 refers specifically to Jesus' exorcisms and healings; and v. 34 highlights the role of Jesus as Protector of the City, a common attribution of secular saviors.

As explained earlier, a reputation for power in word was the counterpart to beneficent action and therefore a cardinal feature in consideration of one who was considered a benefactor or person of exceptional merit. In keeping with his association of hazard with performance in the course of Jesus' ministry, Luke notes various negative reactions to the words of Jesus. Included in this category are 11:37–54; 15:1–2; 16:1–14; 19:47—20:47; 21:37—22:6.

Delegate Benefactors

In Simon's boat Jesus picks up the first members of his cabinet, and Simon and his fishing companions shift to a two-legged species (5:10). Subsequently he who had turned his back on all the authority offered him by the Pseudo-benefactor gives his selected twelve "apostles" (6:13–16) power and authority over the forces of his chief antagonist (9:1), with instructions to proclaim the new politics (9:2). And no deals (v. 5)! Dependent completely on their Benefactor (v. 3), the proclaimers of the New Age proceed, like Joshua's army, to take over the whole land.

As a rhetorical dress rehearsal for his description in Acts of the worldwide mission, Luke recites another royal embassy, this time consisting of thirty-five or thirty-six teams, two each (10:1–20). Benefactors under the Great Benefactor, they are to heal the sick and proclaim the presence of God's reign (v. 9). The power play worked. Tumbled from the heights (10:18–19), Satan feels the impact of the promise in the Magnificat (1:52). As for the Seventy, they are reminded that their responsibility is to be benefactors, not power brokers.

Paul, with the credentials of a Servant-Benefactor, will continue the bombardment (Acts 26:17-18). Such is the authority of the proclaimers of the gospel that there is little distinction between the description of their mission and that of Jesus. Benefactors all, God, the Highest Authority of all, takes any rejection of their persons as a personal affront (Luke 10:16).

As participants in the politics of the New Age, the emissaries of the Great Benefactor are not left to their own clever resources. They will play no games with their adversaries. And if they share in the power of their own Benefactor, they will also share hazards that befall him. He did not ask less of his followers (see 12:4-7; 18:29-30) than citizens were wont to offer to the Caesars. The oath of the Paphlagonians spares nothing for Caesar Augustus and his family:

I swear . . . that in whatever concerns their advantage I am prepared to spare neither my body [sōma] nor life [psychē], nor livelihood [bios], nor children [tekna], and will endure [hypomenō] any danger in behalf of their interests. . . .[20]

As was the case with Jesus, so the followers of Jesus will be brought before the high courts of religion and the state. But they are not to be concerned about diplomatic speech. Freed for the possibilities of the moment, the Holy Spirit will direct their choice of words (Luke 12:11-12). In keeping with his technique of involving the life of Jesus in the ongoing life of Christians, Luke incorporates such words in anticipation of the freedom of speech described from the beginning to the end of Acts (2:29 through 26:26). And most appropriately Luke closes his two-volume work with a description of Paul proclaiming the kingdom of God and teaching about the Lord Jesus Christ with complete freedom of speech—and this under the very nose of Caesar! In Luke's book, all endangered benefactors win.

Benefaction of Peace

One of the principal contributions of a benefactor, as can be seen from the decree concerning Caesar Augustus' birthday, is the bestowal of peace. Therefore it is no surprise that Luke uses the term for peace (see also the fulsome preamble by Tertullus, Acts 24:2-3) in his Gospel more often than do the other three evangelists combined. Thus Luke 1:79 finds an echo in Simeon's words (2:29-32), which in turn echo the association of terms in 2:11, 14. Such peace, understood primarily as achievement of an intimate relationship between God and the beneficiary of divine largesse, is promised to the sinful woman (7:50) and to her counterpart, the woman with a flow of blood who lived in former isolation from Israel's worshiping community (8:48). Peace is the main cargo of the missionizing church (10:5-6). Along the route of widespread proclamation of the good news, traditional expectations of national deliverance (1:68-71) take on new form. Some copyists who caught the spirit of Luke's theme assigned the word to Jesus' first post-resurrection greeting to his huddled followers (24:36).

Peace Rejected

As Joshua warned the immigrants to Canaan, peace can be fragile, and they could lose their land (Josh. 23:15–16). With the help of such thematic precedent and warning, Luke endeavored to revalidate the depressed credentials of Jesus. It was not an easy task. The prophet Zechariah was popular among sponsors of apocalyptic hope, and this prophet had said that God would *visit* (Zech. 10:3) the flock of Judah and Jerusalem would be the citadel of the world. If Jesus was the Messiah, why did he permit his own capital city to fall in the year 70? Already in 2:34 Luke had signaled the disastrous consequences of God's attempt to share peace with the world: "The thoughts of many hearts would be revealed" as Jesus became a sign that would be under attack. In his directions to the Seventy (10:5–6) he prepared his emissaries for hostility and said: "Whatever house you approach, say to the family, 'Peace!' If they want the message you have to offer, the gain will be theirs. If not, take your good news to the next place." Acts 13:46; 28:20 echo the dominical words.

To demonstrate where the responsibility lies for the failure to realize the benefit of peace, Luke combines in 11:21–26 an illustration about security measures with a case history of demonic repossession. Through this editorial association and amplification of synoptic material (see Mark 3:27; Matt. 12:29–30, 43–45) Luke is able to sharpen for his public the point of the illustration about the strong man and the stronger. Luke has already cleared the way for his interpretation of the dominical saying by taking the story about Beelzebul out of its context in Mark 3 and putting it back-to-back with a pericope that concentrates on divine donation of the Holy Spirit (Luke 11:1–13). Thus the good and the evil spirit are contrasted. Similarly 11:21–26 speaks of a good and a bad condition. Only now the point is emphasized that allegiance to Jesus spells the difference. Those who accuse Jesus of being in league with Beelzebul are like a person whose house is secure only so long as a stronger one does not attack it. Actually it is they, not Jesus, who are in league with the demonic world. They think that by virtue of their adherence to Mosaic and other tradition they are "clean." But the former demonic tenant sees the possibilities in clean quarters and brings in seven seamier roommates.

In keeping with the same theme, Luke records words that are in express contradiction to the hope expressed in 1:17, yet in harmony with Micah 7:6: "Do you think I have come to offer peace on the earth? Absolutely not—I bring division" (12:51). Such a statement is in harmony with the actual situation experienced in the Christian mission and Luke again confirms the validity of Jesus' credentials by indicting the culprits responsible for such domestic warfare. Good at weather reports, they are oblivious to the moment of decision that is present in the person and proclamation of Jesus Christ. Most poignantly the contrast between what is and might have been is brought to expression in 19:38 and 42. The message of the church is the promise of peace recited in v. 38. But "some Pharisees" object to the connection of Israel's eschatological hope with the name of Jesus. Thus they have only themselves to blame, suggests Luke, for the nonfulfillment of prophetic dreams for Jerusalem. They failed to perceive the "things that pertained to their peace," and the city that was promised supremacy in the world is leveled to the ground (vv. 42–44). Zechariah 14:21 had said that in the prosperous days to come no trader would be seen in the house of the Lord. Luke concludes Jesus' dire forecast of Jerusalem's fate with the recital of his expulsion of the traders from the temple. Jesus' action on the one hand confirms his credentials, for he is the Messiah of the end time, but the activity of the traders beclouds the real function of the temple and further seals Jerusalem's fate.

Peace for the World

Next to peace, Israel's major benefit under Joshua was possession of the land of Canaan, and some of Luke's public, exposed to Luke 19:38, could not fail to note that Zechariah's (9:9) description of the victorious king of Jerusalem riding on an ass went hand in hand with promise of a rule that was to extend to the farthest reaches of the earth (v. 10). With the fall of Jerusalem all hope of fulfillment seemed to evaporate. But Simeon's description of Jesus as "light for the revelation of the gentiles" and "the glory of Israel" finds realization in the proclamation of forgiveness of sins to all the nations (24:47).

From a monument at Ankara, capital city of Galatia, Caesar Augustus proclaimed: "In victory I spared all citizens who begged for mercy. Foreign nations, where it was safe to grant clemency, I preferred to spare rather than to annihilate."[21] Imitating the clemency of which Julius Caesar boasted, Augustus recited for the ages the highest benefaction that a ruler can bestow. But the forgiveness proclaimed in the name of Jesus was far more global.

Conclusion

A basic question can now be answered. In what way is Jesus distinguished from all other benefactors, and how would Luke's non-Jewishly oriented Greco-Roman public perceive the distinction? Greco-Roman perceptions of exceptional human benefactors known as immortals provide a primary clue. Among the most firmly established were Herakles, Dionysos, Aristaios, and Romulus, the first ruler of Rome. High on the list of others who enjoyed such prestige, albeit with varying degrees of support, were Pythagoras, Plato, Alexander the Great, Julius Caesar, and Caesar Augustus. Extraordinary portents attend their rise to glory.[22]

As one who is more than mortal, in the Greco-Roman world Jesus would be understood as possessing the kinds of powers that magicians aspired to control, with a view to conferring benefits on their clients. Luke's interest in celebrating Jesus' far superior faculties is apparent from his description of an encounter between Christian missionaries and the magicians Simon (Acts 8:9-25) and Elymas (Acts 13:6-12). Marvels that are traditionally associated with magicians' spells play an important role in Luke's work: for example, control of natural phenomena (Luke 8:22-25; 17:6); levitation (Acts 8:39-40); opening of locked quarters (5:19-21; 12:6-10; 16:26); exorcisms (Luke 4:35; 8:29; 9:42); and healings (5:13; 7:14; 17:14; 18:42) at command. Also, as Acts 19:13-17 attests, magic in the wrong hands can backfire.

Also from the manner in which Luke records the circumstances surrounding especially the birth and death of Jesus, Luke's public would readily grasp that Jesus belonged to a class of supra-exceptional benefactors. But it remained for Luke to interpret his unique status. Much of Luke's use of Jesus' names and titles and discussions related to them have a bearing on the question (for our detailed analysis, see chap. 5 of this book). Here it is necessary only to refer again to Acts 4:8-12. Having established that the healing (the verb is cognate with the noun for salvation) falls into the category of benefaction (v. 9), Luke shows that Peter and John are mere instruments for the display of God's beneficence that is authorized through appeal to the name of Jesus. The evangelist concludes the passage with Peter's definitive statement concerning the one name: "Salvation is to be found in no other. In all the world there is no one else whom God has given to save us" (v. 12). Not all benefactors are saviors, but all saviors are benefactors. Yet not all saviors are chosen to confer God's singular benefit of salvation. Jesus alone qualifies for the task. He is the Superstar of superstars. All human beings are God's offspring (17:28), but Jesus is the unique Son of God. It comes as no surprise, then, that the word "today" is one of Luke's favorite words (21 times in Luke-Acts; see especially Luke 2:11; 19:9), and that the shepherds at Bethlehem (2:16) and Zacchaeus at Jericho (19:5) came with haste into the Great Benefactor's presence.

CHAPTER FOUR

REVERSAL OF FORTUNES

Luke's Dramatic Imagination

The second major indicator of Luke's ability to probe Greek, as well as Jewish, experience, is his mastery of the theme of altered or reversed fortunes (*peripeteia*). Awareness of this theme, in its negative as well as positive form, will offer students ready entree to apprehension of meanings in Luke's work.

It is no literary accident that Greeks developed drama to a high art five centuries before Luke wrote his story. Homer had laid the groundwork for exploration of the dramatic possibilities in his descriptions of good fortune that gives way to calamity. Human beings against the forces of destiny and a variety of divine counsels, with occasional reversals in favor of the sufferer. This was the action on a spacious stage.

Termed "peripeteia" by Greeks, this fundamental human experience finds classic treatment in Sophokles' *King Oidipous*. After solving the riddle posed by the Sphinx, Oidipous won the right to govern Thebes. But his desire to probe the riddle of his own life drove him beyond the boundaries of the golden mean. Inattentive to the warnings of the blind prophet Teresias, Oidipous keeps on probing and ultimately discovers that he murdered his father and married his own mother. Overcome by the horror of his deeds he puts out his eyes. Two millenia later John Milton captured the point in a few lines, when he wrote in reference to another solver of riddles:

> Behold this great deliverer now,
> Eyeless in Gaza, at a mill with slaves.

Life does indeed play a multitude of bane-filled tricks. And no one surpassed Homer in sympathetic expression. He bids us look at the princess Andromache, once a queen in Hektor's palace and now, in her own words, a slave in the house of Achilles. Endurance is what it takes, proclaimed the same blind bard about the fortunes of Odysseus.

Others would embalm the perception in clichés. "The best thing is never to have been born." So spoke the Koheleths of Hellas. *Sōphrosynē* (moderation, prudence) is the road to take, pontificated the less morbid. *Mēden agan*, nothing to excess, made philosophers out of stone masons.

"Judge no one happy until death," Solon counselled Croesus. And he underscored the lesson with these words: "One who dies well has lived well" (Herodotos 1.32.5). Prosperity or satiety (*koros*) is hazardous, especially to a person who is deficient in character, for it can promote insolence (*hybris*), which invites ruinous retribution (*atē*). Roman writers, imitators of things Greek, picked up the thought: "Look at life's last lap," advised Juvenal (10:274–75).

Beyond individual fortunes is humanity's corporate fate. The very first chapters of Genesis give expression to its lament over the loss of a golden time. This Hebrew perception of corporate peripeteia is part of a network of profound brooding that stretches across the entire Mediterranean world. In Greece it found expression in Hesiod's myth of the ages (*Works and Days*), with variations in Plato's *Republic* and in modern times in such thoughts as the one expressed by playwright David Mamet in "An Embarrassment of Liberty." After sketching the loss of national reputation at home and abroad, he concludes, "We have become a warmonger nation" that is "dedicated to the proliferation of arms," who would "rather die than examine, let alone alter, our image of ourselves as just, all-seeing, always right." Like tragic heroes, we "appropriate . . . the attributes of God . . . and we must and do suffer."[1]

Awareness of a common fund of understanding in antiquity concerning human destiny suggests a partial answer to the reason why Luke's writing became a classic in its own right. He could count on understanding from a broad range of publics. Even the very first chapters of Luke's Gospel—not to speak of numerous other parts of his two-volume work—would, despite so much of their admittedly Hebrew flavor, project for Greco-Roman auditors the somber strains of their own seers, the poets.

So many dreams struggle for fulfillment. Luke knows well how to reach humanity's heart. Barren Elizabeth finally bears a child. John is his name, and he will turn "many of the children of Israel to the Lord their God," reports the divine messenger. Once he has assumed his obligation, John "will reconcile fathers to their children, and he will cause the disobedient to change their ways" (1:17). Gabriel, distinguished messenger, declares that Jesus the Great will "be given the throne of his ancestor David, and he will reign forever over the house of Jacob" (1:32–33). A startling declaration, for outside Jewish boundaries eternity was reserved for Rome.

Magnificat

Then comes the Magnificat, only now the peripeteia is double-edged. The rise of one spells the fall of another. "God scatters the proud, . . . brings down the mighty, and elevates the oppressed . . ." (1:51–52). At first hearing we think we catch an echo from the words of the Greek poet Archilochos:

> The deities are ever just. Full oft they raise
> those who lie prostrate on the darkened earth.
> Full oft the prosperous are tripped, their bellies

to the sky; and miseries untold attend them.
Mindless, in aimless poverty they wander.[2]

But the rest of Luke's poem points to a profound difference in perspectives. Besides Archilochos, many other Hellenes wrote about divine "fairness." Life is chancey, they say, and the deities take no account of status. But at least no one can say, "The gods pick on me." But in Archilochos's lines the destinies of the mighty and the lowly are not defined from a moral perspective, nor are they conceptualized in terms of an adversarial relationship.

Luke prefers to stress the kind of correction that Aischylos offered to the over-simplified version that misery is the necessary counterpart to prosperity. In the *Agamemnon* (462–67) Aischylos shows how the Erinyes destroy those who are prosperous without justice. In Luke's Magnificat it is evident that divine intervention must take place because entrenched interests have not discharged their obligations to the less powerful. The result of God's intervention will therefore spell a reversal in fortunes for both the oppressor and the oppressed.

The precise identity of the oppressors and of the oppressed remains to be established. Most of Luke's auditors, of course, can be presumed to know who these are (cf. Luke 22:25–27). But the Greco-Romans among them bring their perspective of peripeteia to the audition and grasp the dramatic moment. One can be guilty of *hybris*. Those acquainted with the Hebrew Scriptures would know that prophets had warned about misuse of the privilege of election as God's people. What will happen now, when God's promises present themselves for fulfillment, as they have in connection with Jesus, who is shortly to be born of Mary?

Benedictus

Zachariah's song, the Benedictus (1:68–79), amplifies the promise of the Magnificat. Corporate hope, with remembrance of things past and dreams of restoration, here finds expression. And interpreters who are sensitive to the atmosphere of peripeteia that surrounds the text know that they must restrain themselves from spiritualizing the poem along individualistic lines. Luke gives full-throated utterance to the notes that sound the music of the Golden Age Restored. Against their background, the ruinous realities to come burst forth with arresting tonality. The mighty will be brought low and the lowly will be exalted, but in a way never dreamed by many who thought that their places were assured in the New Age.

Birth of Jesus

The dream of restoration comes to climactic expression in the announcement of the birth of Jesus. Once again the thought of peace, the dominant feature of any new age, finds expression (2:14). God is well pleased. The line of thought espoused by Archilochos has received its full revision. One can count on the divine attitude. It is one of committed beneficence.

Luke's auditors know how the story ends, and in the context of fullness of divine generosity Greco-Romans among them would think about *hybris* (insolence) and *atē* (retribution). As they linked the angelic message to the shepherds with all the other words of promise that preceded it, they would recollect that life corroborates the truth of Solon's words. Proud Jerusalem, with her beautiful temple, lies in ruins. On the other hand, precisely because they know the full story, they do not think that a Solon has spoken the last word. Jesus is the key to the whole. And so they are ready to hear Simeon's assessment: "This one lies for the rising and falling of many in Israel" (2:34).

Reversal in Luke's Story Line

At the point of Simeon's entry into the narrative there appears to be a sudden switch in story lines. It is no longer Israel and her opposition, but *a division of the house* within Israel that surfaces in Luke's narrative. This alteration is itself a peripeteia. And Jesus, instead of masterminding the program of restoration, himself shares in the reversal cycle by incorporating in his own experience the proverbial realities. He, Jesus the Great, is himself headed for a peripeteia: "A broadsword shall go through your own heart" is the word to his mother, Mary (2:35). From this point on, Luke's auditors will think in terms of the ideal possibility for Israel and also its disastrous denial of greatness. The contrast constitutes the dramatic core of Luke's book, which has the major ingredients of tragedy. Both Jesus and Israel's leadership are intensely devoted to God, but their difference in approach puts them on a collision course. From a purely Greek perspective, both exceed the ideal of *mēden agan* ("nothing to excess") and deserve their fate, which appears to confirm Solon's maxim.

Upon the appearance of John in the wilderness, the reversal beat is unmistakable. God can raise up descendants for Abraham out of the very stones (3:9), the implication being that others fall. The thought is reinforced at v. 17 in the contrast of grain and chaff.

At the Mount of Temptation, the devil offers to elevate Jesus to a post higher than that of a Caesar (4:5-8). Jesus declines, and the refusal will be costly, for Simeon's prophetic awareness is echoed at v. 13. The devil awaits the time (see 22:3) when he will be able to topple Jesus. But during the interval Jesus assumes the initiative, and Luke's auditors will hear 10:18 declaring the ultimate failure of Satan's effort to discredit Jesus.

In his inaugural address at Nazareth (4:16-30) the reversal motif is sounded in two strains. The poor, the captives, the blind, and the bruised can look forward to a new day (vv. 18-19). But trouble is on the way for others. In contrast to the many, one leper and one widow in Israel's ancient time were beneficiaries of prophetic intervention. Luke's auditors know from the way in which Luke tells his story that Sidon (v. 26) and Syria (v. 27) must lie outside Israel's territory. Many will one day flock from all directions, and the insiders will be looking in from the outside (13:28).

Capernaum's privileged position is noted at 4:23, and at 10:16 its fall is announced. Woes are pronounced on self-esteemed arbiters of tradition (11:42-52). Those who build the tombs of the prophets and thereby affirm their hope of security in tradition will find themselves liable for the blood of all the prophets from Abel to Zachariah (11:46-51). The warning is repeated in 13:1-6. Yes, they could be forgiven, even for the shedding of prophets' blood, but they prevent any possibility of absolution (13:34-35). And because of their self-exaltation they must hear the doom-filled maxim of 14:11: "All those who exalt themselves will be abased, and those who humble themselves will be exalted." And in the end, the stone that is rejected will reverse the prestige of those who disqualified it (20:9-18).

There is no end of peripeteia! Ordinary fishers and a publican named Levi become privileged partners of the New Age Deliverer (5:1-11, 27-32); a leper joins Naaman in receipt of healing (vv. 12-16); a paralytic (vv. 17-26) becomes the beneficiary of forgiveness that was announced at Nazareth; and another sufferer has his hand restored to usefulness (6:6-11). Jesus calls a halt to a widow's lamentations (7:11-17). And a notorious woman is raised to honorable status (7:36-50).

Disciples of Jesus are granted insight into the mysteries of God, whereas others see worse and hear worse after exposure to parables (8:9-10; 10:21-24).

Outsiders become insiders and insiders become outsiders (8:19-20; 13:23-30). A man who was shunted to the tombs is restored to society (8:26-39), and a woman enjoys full status as a daughter of God after being cut off for twelve years from the corporate religious life of Israel (vv. 43-48).

Willingness to share the ignominy of Jesus wins life; short-sighted saving of one's life guarantees its loss (9:23-27; cf. 17:33). Those who make public affirmation of Jesus will have status in the heavenly court; those who make public denial of him will lose it (12:8-9). The least become the great (9:48; 18:15-17).

Current connections are no guarantee of entry in the end-time social register (13:23-30). A multitude of social misfits receives an invitation to a banquet, and the original guest list is scrapped (14:16-24). Despite the warning issued by John (3:18), a certain rich man claimed Abraham as his father. Champion enticer of the *koros-hybris-atē* syndrome, he makes his claim an astounding three times (16:24, 27, 30) and therewith personally assures himself a place in the pain-filled area of Hades. Zacchaeus made no claim on the genealogy and was issued a coat of arms by Jesus (19:9).

In Luke 15 a young man goes from riches to rags and back again, and in

16:1–9 a crooked manager catches himself in a fall from his position and wins a circle of friends. Lazarus goes from poverty to the height of social status (16:19–23), and Jesus assures his disciples of a similar reversal (18:28–30). But a rich man declines to join the ranks of the poor and loses all (18:18–23). Kings on occasion offer half their kingdom to a favorite, but the kingdom of God is granted without restriction to all who surmount the cares of this life (12:22–34).

Ten lepers are healed, but only one is told, "Rise up and go. Your faith has rescued you" (17:19). On the day that the Son of humanity is revealed, "one will be taken and the other left" (17:34–35). So it was in the temple, when two men went to pray (18:9–14). Some adults will discover that children take precedence at the entrance to the kingdom (18:15–17). Just before the entry into Jerusalem, Jesus declares that those who have get more, and those who have nothing to speak of will lose even what they have (19:26).

A despised son of David is elevated and his enemies are overthrown (20:41–44). Hated followers of Jesus will ultimately triumph (21:12–28). From a self-assured and assuring stance (22:33) Peter takes a sorrowful plunge (vv. 54–62), but Jesus arranges for another reversal (v. 32). Finally, at the crucifixion one of two lawbreakers gains assurance of paradise (23:43).

According to Acts 1:17–20, Judas falls from his privileged position. Ananias and Sapphira pay a macabre price for not taking the Holy Spirit seriously (5:1–11). And Stephen's speech (Acts 7), which echoes Luke 20:9–18, is a series of vignettes that describe the varying fortunes of Joseph, Moses, and Israel. Luke's rationale for ending his two-volume work as he does will be discussed below.

Besides passages in which the fall or rising of individuals or groups is quite apparent, there are numerous instances in which a division of the house is simply reported. That is, some accept the message and others reject it, with the implication that the latter are the losers. References in Luke's Gospel to opposition from representatives of Israel's religious establishment are especially illustrative of the category. See, for example, 5:22 (with its apparent reminiscence of 2:35); 7:30; 11:14–54; 15:1–32 (the elder brother); 16:14–17; 19:45–48; and 22:1–6.

In Acts the opposition aspect is set forth initially at 2:12–13, and shortly thereafter priests and Sadducees express their chagrin over the proclamation of the resurrection in connection with Jesus (Acts 4:1–37). Their hostility intensifies to such extent (5:17–32) that a Pharisee named Gamaliel warns them against the possibility of their engagement in a perilous error of judgment (vv. 33–39). Stephen's proclamations (6:8—7:53) lead to his execution by stoning, with Paul billed as a supporter of the Sanhedrin's decision (vv. 54–60).

According to Luke's report at 8:26–39, a eunuch becomes a privileged recipient of the benefits of the New Age. To those of Luke's auditors who were familiar with Isa. 56:1-5, his experience suggests an anastatic or turn-for-the-better strain, which not only reverses discriminatory exclusion of eunuchs from the congregation of Israel (see Lev. 22:24; Deut. 23:1), but gives them an edge over unfaithful Israelites.

After Saul's conversion, there is a division of the house concerning him (9:23-25). At Pisidian Antioch two factions develop over the proclamation made by Paul and Barnabas (13:42-48). A similar experience awaits them at Iconium (14:1-6). After his separation from Barnabas, Paul goes on with Silas to Greece, where they encounter a division at Thessalonika (17:1-9). The inhospitable party at that city in turn contrasts with a more open-minded element at Beroia (vv. 10-13).

Upon the completion of a presentation at Athens, Paul encounters mockery as well as a positive response (17:32-34). At Corinth many of the Jews reject Paul's message, but the head of the synagogue takes his entire household into the new household of faith (18:5-8). After speaking freely for three months in a synagogue at Ephesos, Paul is forced out by Jews and sets up headquarters at the school of one named Tyrannos, where Jews as well as Greeks listen to his message (19:8-10). A division of the house also develops at Jerusalem, when Pharisees and Sadducees brawl with one another over Paul's resurrection message (23:6-10). At Luke 2:34, Simeon spoke about the sign that is "spoken against" (*antilegō*). In a striking echo of the Greek verb at Acts 28:22, Luke has Jewish leaders in Rome observe that the Christians are "everywhere . . . spoken against." Further discussion of the climactic division that took place at Rome (28:24) is offered below.

In a related category are those who miss their opportunity. Notable among them are the ruler who asked what he might do to inherit eternal life (18:18-23), Judas (Acts 1:15-20), the unrepentant malefactor (Luke 23:39), and Ananias and Sapphira (Acts 5:1-11).

Now-Then Motif

Special attention must be paid to a common Greek literary feature in statements of reversal. The basic component is the adverb *nyn* (now), which is frequently, but not necessarily, balanced by *tote* (then) or an equivalent expression. In the absence of the second component, the writer's publics are expected to make the appropriate inference.

Homer helped to institutionalize the now-then motif as a literary device in Hellenic circles. In the *Iliad* (18:57-60), Thetis, mother of Achilles, expresses the heart of all mothers who have sent their sons to war, when she mourns in dread foreboding and balances the heroic virtues of Achilles against the pain that will soon be hers when he can never return to her again:

> I nurtured him, a tender plant within a fruitful field.
> In beaked ships I sent him forth to Ilium's coast,

> to fight the hosts of Troy. But I can greet no more
> my warrior when he makes his way to Pelian's hearth.

At the sight of Achilles' friend Patroklos, quiet in death, the captive daughter of Briseis gives utterance to what all female slaves have ever thought in the face of a loss that once more puts their lives at risk:

> O Patroklos, strength of my heart in sorrow's hour.
> When within I left our couch, I saw you alive.
> But now, O leader of the people, I find you here
> laid out in death. What woe upon woe is my fate![3]

According to Athenaeus, the tragedian Aischylos confessed that his dramas were sliced from Homer's board. In the *Agamemnon* the chorus reflects on the waste of life at Troy and views the men who have gone off to war in contrast to their present circumstance—a little weight of ashes (lines 434–44).

In the *Prometheus,* the hero expresses the wish that he had been secured in Tartaros rather than be exposed for all to see. As it is, he now provides sport for his enemies (153–59). The phrase *nyn de* highlights the contrast between the present misery of exposure and insult and the hidden punishment of his sin that he would have preferred.

To open the dramatic storehouses of Sophokles and Euripides for exhibition of their use of the then-now motif would amount to transport of marble to Paros. This is not to say that Greeks had a monopoly on the thought. A Babylonian poem, "The Righteous Sufferer," notes the rapidity with which the contrast can take place:

> He who was alive yesterday is dead today.
> For a minute he was dejected, suddenly he is exuberant.
> One moment people are singing in exaltation,
> another they groan like professional mourners.[4]

A Chinese poet, Chang Tsai, of the third century in our era, expressed the thought in its baldest form:

> They that were once lords of a thousand hosts
> are now become the dust of the hills and ridges.
> I think of what Yun-men said
> and I am sorely grieved at the thought of "then" and "now."[5]

In Luke's work the then-now feature is strikingly present in the Sermon on the Plain—and especially so in formulation of the blessings and the woes (6:20–26)—where Luke's carefully paired structure would have unmistakably conveyed to his Greco-Roman auditors a variation of the rise-fall motif that was commonly expressed in terms of "now" and "then."

In his narrative of the rich man and Lazarus (16:19–31) Luke gives the theme an exceptionally striking expression. His narrative contains much Jewish flavor, but Greco-Romans have easy port of entry through the vivid description of Hades and the feature of then-and-now. The contrast that was earlier expressed in the Sermon on the Plain is unmistakable in this narrative, with the particle *nyn* (16:25) signalling the rich man's tragedy and the poor man's comedy.

One of the most dramatic instances of Luke's use of the then-now formulation is 19:42, in which Jesus contrasts what might have been with the dreadful reality that is on its way. Indicative of Luke's Hellenic consciousness is his use of a conditional formulation. This device of stating a wish regarding the past and then contrasting it with a juxtaposed statement about present or imminent calamity finds expression in Sophokles' formulation of an antiphonal lament by the hero of *King Oidipous* (1360–63). In contrast to what might have been, he mourns:

> But now (*nyn de*) I am ignored by God, an unholy offspring,
> wed to one from whom I, a wretch, was born.

Overt then-now diction need not be present to catch a Greco-Roman auditor's attention. The story of the rich man narrated in 12:16–21 is generated by the basic language of then-and-now. At the moment of his apparent triumph over all obstacles to his security, the rich man is his own victim of the *koros-hybris-atē* syndrome and verifies the truth of a proverb that was cited in another context: "Those who seek to save their lives will lose them" (9:24). An especially lurid example of the syndrome appears in Acts 12:20–26. Perched on a pinnacle of popularity, Herod Agrippa I forgets his mortality and invites a shocking end for himself.

Fall and Rise of Jesus

In the case of Jesus, Greco-Roman auditors would have been intrigued by the fact that Jesus, acclaimed as the Son of God, suffered an ignominious death despite the fact that he was completely upright (*dikaios*) and had always deferred to God. His fall, therefore, could not be attributed to some fault within himself, some violation of *mēden agan*. But was he, perchance, the victim of cosmic caprice? Perhaps of the type that Nausikaa spoke of when she consoled Odysseus with the thought that, without always taking account of desert (*Odyssey* 6:188–90), God dispenses happiness and woe to both the good and to the evil? From the manner in which the evangelist concludes his narrative Luke's auditors would hear a vehement "no" to such speculations. And from the declarations of woe and many types of warnings expressed earlier at various points in Luke's Gospel, they would be prepared for understanding of the denouement.

Precisely in the intersection of the experience of the "many" and of the one who is proclaimed as Savior Luke provides the counterthrust to Solon's estimate of human experience. Jesus goes to his death in full knowledge of its circumstances, and he does so out of obedience to his heavenly Parent, who risks everything to remain faithful to the oath that was made with Abraham (1:73). From his eminence as the Son of God (1:35) he does indeed fall to the lowest depths, but God raises Jesus from the dead and declares him Christ and Lord despite the efforts that were made to discredit him (Acts 2:36; cf. Luke 2:11, 26). The cause of his fall is, in Luke's judgment, Jesus' own people, who subject him to what Simeon predicted in 2:35.

By bringing about the fall of Jesus the hostile forces threaten themselves with a fall from the glorious destiny that can be theirs (see 2:32). But even Israel as a totality, guilty as she was of bringing about the apparent downfall of Jesus the Great, is offered the opportunity to rise from her self-humiliation. In association with Jesus, God proclaims forgiveness to those who shared responsibility for his crucifixion (2:38), thereby giving them the opportunity to avoid real tragedy and to be the beneficiaries of the rising that was promised at Luke 2:32 (see Acts 2:37–42). Jesus is not the tragic figure. Those who do not heed the apostolic proclamation of amnesty are the ones who ultimately compose their own tragedy.

Because Luke crafted his narrative so carefully, it was not necessary to state explicitly that Jerusalem had fallen. Instead, he suggests the disaster through various prophecies and allusions and permits his auditors to bring the specific information with them to the hearing of his narrative. Through their exposure to his story the disaster becomes not only a part of history but the substance of tragic narration.

Similarly, the ending of Acts is appropriate from a literary perspective. It is not necessary to infer that, because Luke does not record the death of Paul, he must have written both before the fall of Jerusalem and before the apostle's demise. The literary design is that Paul, who once fell from the heights of Pharisaic piety, should rise to become the apostle to the Gentiles and reach Rome in the course of his obligation. There also he is to encounter what Simeon prophesied—the "rise and fall of many in Israel" (28:24–25).

This interpretation of Luke's appeal to dramatic imagination is not invalidated by the probability averred by some that Luke might have written before the fall of Jerusalem. In such case, Greco-Roman auditors, especially those steeped in Jewish biblical tradition, would simply have expected fulfillment of the third component of the *koros-hybris-atē* syndrome, even as Scipio is said to have pondered the ultimate destruction of Rome when he surveyed his ruinous handiwork at smoldering Carthage. Certainly from a literary perspective, then, it is not important to know whether Jerusalem has actually fallen or not. The fact is that Luke, whether with a Hebrew or Greek spirit, writes as one who knows what the end of such a city must be, and he can count on his auditors to do the same. Luke's plot has its own integrity, and any observations of a latter-day interpreter that appear to be based on imported historical assumptions can be transposed into dramatic literary anticipation. Nor does such awareness of literary probabilities denigrate the prophetic feature in Luke's record of Jesus' words. Combined with the inherent integrity of Luke's plot, the prophetic element serves as powerful reinforcement of the dominating theme of divine control of history (1:1).

PART 3

"NO OTHER NAME"

CHAPTER FIVE

JESUS—CHRIST AND LORD

Luke's Task

"Benefactor" is the primary model that Luke's Greco-Roman publics would bring to the hearing of a work that featured a person of such exceptional merit as Jesus was proclaimed to be. Viewing Jesus as the Great Benefactor, they would be able to follow debates involving numerous questions about Jesus' identity and function and they would grasp some of the meaning that came more readily to their Jewish friends through such terms as "Messiah," "Son of David," "Son of God," "Son of humanity (man)," "Christ," and "Lord." Indeed, Luke's ability to probe issues about the Christ in a way that was meaningful to both Hellenic and Jewish publics is his chief claim to fame as a writer. After all, *"all* the people" came to hear Jesus (21:38), and *"all* the people hung upon his words" (19:48).

That "Christ" and "Lord" are Luke's favorite titles for Jesus can be statistically determined, but Luke himself (2:11) explicitly alerts his readers to the fact by defining the word *sōtēr* (Savior) as equivalent to *christos kyrios* (Messiah Lord). The passage finds echo in Acts 2:36: "Therefore, let every Israelite know beyond a doubt that it is God who has made him Lord and Messiah." Whatever may have been earliest Christianity's understanding of the Christ, Luke himself in this passage did not say that Jesus became something after his resurrection that he had not been before. Luke says that Jesus who was crucified had his credentials as Messiah and Lord verified and amplified by the resurrection (see also Acts 5:31). Despite attempts to disqualify Jesus, God was determined to affirm his credentials.

In the same breath, then, with his stress on the titles Christ and Lord, Luke suggests that the emergence of these two titles represents a triumph over much misunderstanding relating to the person of Jesus of Nazareth. Such misunderstanding would have been especially acute after the destruction of Jerusalem (A.D. 70) when the Christian community was subject to renewed fragmentation. It is difficult to imagine the impact that the destruction of Jerusalem must have had on Christians who had to relocate. The shock waves would penetrate every Christian outpost, and scavenging wolves, who come in the wake of any disaster, would prey on people's fears, ignorance, and anxiety (cf. Acts 20:18–30).

From Luke's two-volume work, Luke-Acts, it is easy to reconstruct some of the questions that would be asked. Was the city destroyed because the faith of the fathers, Abraham and Isaac and Jacob, had been sabotaged? Were people too quick to follow Jesus, thinking he was the Messiah, when after all he may merely have been another prophet, and misguided at that? And what about some of the things he said, including his claim that people around him would not die before they had seen the kingdom of God (Luke 9:27)? Is it really wise to continue allegiance to Jesus of Nazareth, who was crucified as an insurgent slave? Perhaps one "like a son of humanity," as described by Daniel, will come and God will solve all our problems. What sense can some of our neighbors make of the resurrection of the body?

One can conclude from these theoretical musings how complicated Luke's task was. Unfortunately, as modern readers we lack the live controversial context in which Luke's literary statement of the issues could be readily understood. Moreover, Luke does not present us with an analytical account in which the parties are clearly defined and developments carefully traced. Keeping authorial intrusion to a minimum, Luke for the most part relates stories and conversations. But the skill of ancient rhetoricians—and historical writing was a branch of rhetoric—displayed itself in arrangement of the material; and from the manner in which traditions are handled one can make reasonably accurate inferences concerning the author's lines of thought. Apart from Luke's own tipping of his editorial hand, we are able to compare his modifications of parallel texts and traditions, Mark and Q, as controls for our study.

As an anchor for the apostolic faith, Luke appeals to the traditional sacred writings, which were familiar in their Hellenistic expanded form to Jews and Gentiles in the lands of the dispersion. Luke's referral to the Greek form of the OT text reflects in the main the version known as the Septuagint, which includes writings not included in the Hebrew canon. Among these writings, *Wisdom* and *Sirach,* characterized as sapiential, are especially pertinent for study of Luke's writings.

Fundamental to Luke's presentation of Jesus' credentials is the sapiential view of the divine goodness that permeates all of God's dealings with humanity. Jesus is the supreme manifestation of God's goodness, for in the face of rejection by God's own people, God restored him to his nation, and through that nation to all humanity.

What God has done in the case of Jesus is in keeping with God's activity and sense of frustration in the past. Acts 7 reflects in one substantial literary unit the kind of river of thought out of which much of Luke's christological expression springs. Developed along the same formal lines as Psalm 77 (78) and *Wisdom* 10, this speech (like the parable in Luke 20:9–18) displays the perils confronting divine magnanimity in the course of history and affirms that the legalized assassination of Jesus is of a piece with atrocities committed in the past. But, as always, God has the last word over evil, and the Scriptures, acknowledged expression of the divine will and purpose, are to be used as the ultimate court of appeal in the judgment of christological claims.

God—Maker of Kings: Son of David or Son of God?

At the top of Luke's list of objectives is the proper understanding of Jesus in relation to the national hope revolving around a Davidic heir. With the destruction of Jerusalem, it was difficult to adjust prophetic statements about the cosmic centrality of Jerusalem in the messianic age with its total devastation under Titus in 70, and still more difficult to persuade people that a king who had lost his capital city was nevertheless the Messiah alleged to have ushered in the long-awaited time of peace and security. Therefore, if Luke was to convince his public of the credentials of Jesus for the messianic post, he had to take account of the principal traditions relating to that hope, but in such a way that no sectarian interests would be encouraged. He therefore adopted the rhetorical strategem of letting various traditions appear in tension at the very beginning of his work. Through careful editing he presents in the first two chapters of his Gospel a partial resolution of the conflict in traditions, and then in the rest of his book conducts his auditors into fuller appreciation of the ramifications of the messianic issue.

Of special interest is Luke's handling of traditions relating to the conception and birth of Jesus (1:26-38). Since the messianic age was popularly understood in terms of a golden Davidic age, Luke had to come to terms with such expectations. But failure and disaster were scarcely compatible with the triumphalistic hope. Luke overcomes an apparent impasse by letting stand the traditional interpretation of Jesus' credentials in terms of Davidic fulfillment. Mary is betrothed to Joseph, who is of Davidic blood (1:27).[1]

But before Luke presents the promise concerning the reign of the new David, he emphasizes the prior credentials of Jesus. He will be "great" (*megas*, 1:32). The same expression is used of John at 1:15 (cf. 7:28), but the qualifications ascribed to Jesus in 1:32 point to the superior prestige of the latter. By emphasizing John's greatness, the greatness of Jesus is all the more magnified.

The term "great" was used in the Greek Bible of God (e.g., Deut. 10:17; 1 Chron. 16:25; Mal. 4:1), and of kings (e.g., Isa. 36:4, of Sennacherib; Esther 3:13, of Artaxerxes). And in Jth. 16:16 it is applied to one who fears God. Jewish auditors would probably think of Isa. 9:5-6, with its vision of a Davidic reign of lasting peace. In the Hellenic world the term served as epithet for such deities as Zeus, Demeter, Isis, and Artemis (cf. Acts 19:27-35), and for a few monarchs, including Alexander, Antiochos III, and Demetrios Poliorketes. Listening to the term in the context of Luke 1:32-33, Luke's

Greco-Roman auditors would interpret Jesus not only as a royal benefactor but as one who can lay claim to the extraordinary devotion reserved for deities. If one wished to speak of perpetuity, one would say, "So long as Rome endures." Luke records concerning the reign of Jesus the Great, who will rule "for ever" (cf. 1:33, 54–55).

Since God *gives* him the throne, the royal claim does not belong to Jesus merely on the basis of right of descent, but on God's initiative, who dispenses royalty as seems fit (see 10:22; 22:28–30). Thereby the route is prepared that leads to the statement in Acts 2:36, and vicissitudes of history are no longer the guardians of Jesus' credentials as expected deliverer. Whatever happens to Jerusalem or to the national fortunes of the descendants of Abraham, there will always be an Israel, because God can out of stones create a posterity for Abraham (Luke 3:8), and the reign of Jesus is assured forever.

Jesus' Overt Commitment to the Father

Through the dialogue between Mary and Gabriel, Luke reinforces the uniqueness of Jesus. As later the church, beginning at Pentecost, will owe its existence to the Holy Spirit (Acts 1:8—2:42), so Jesus owes his credentials to the same Spirit, and by virtue of the divine intervention he will qualify as the unique Son of God.

Like the Spirit, who is his divine progenitor, this descendant in David's royal line will be counted "holy" (Luke 1:35). The adjective is carefully chosen, for Jesus will die as one who appears anything but holy. But the apostolic proclamation (see Acts 3:14; 4:27, 30) will set the record straight with echoes of the angel's verdict.

In conformity with such perspective, Luke proceeds to display Jesus' commitment to his heavenly Parent and his acceptance of the route portrayed for him in the Scriptures. A key recital is the story of the twelve-year-old Jesus. Faced with the mystery of his real identity, his mother attempts to fathom the strange disclaimer made at the temple. She had said, "Your father and I have been in tears looking for you." He replied, "Why did you spend so much time looking for me. Didn't you know I had to be in my Father's house?" (Luke 2:49). Thus Luke from the beginning associates Jesus with Jerusalem and with the temple. Beyond question, says Luke, Jesus loved the city and did everything to preserve it. But, as Jesus between sobs warned its inhabitants (19:41–46; cf. 13:34–35), the city invited destruction by denying itself the very instrument of God's security measures. In place of a temple they celebrated a "hideout for thieves" (19:46). Whether God's people were wise in making so much of the temple is a question that Luke takes up later in Acts 7. In his Gospel he is anxious to develop a counterattack against the charge that Jesus was unpatriotic.

Along with avowed devotion to Jerusalem's cultic center, Jesus expresses a profound commitment to his Father's purpose (2:49) in one of Luke's favorite terms, *dei* (it is necessary, I must). This unqualified recognition of his life's assignment is the dynamic aspect of his Sonship and permeates all his activity, including that which came especially under the attack of hostile religionists. As one sent on an official mission, Jesus subsequently declares himself under orders to make his proclamation in many different towns (4:43). The divine urgency extends even to the reception of a despised tax broker, Zacchaeus (19:5). But most frequently the expression of commitment is found in reference to Jesus' ultimate experience in Jerusalem (9:22; 13:33; 17:25; 22:37; and in retrospect, 24:7, 26, 44, 46). To a climactic scene in Luke's description of that last visit we now turn our attention.

"So You Are the Son of God?"

Through his editorial work on the tradition of the trial before the chief priest (22:66–71), Luke displays the theological continuity in Jesus' earlier sense of commitment and his present resolve in the face of what would appear to most observers a shattering of all claims to be Israel's deliverer. Asked by the presbytery whether he is the Messiah (note Luke's deletion here of Mark's reference to the "Son of the Blessed One" = Son of God, Mark 14:61), Jesus speaks of the Son of humanity sitting "from now on at God's powerful right hand." His questioners exclaim, "So then YOU ARE the Son of God?" Jesus replies in the first person singular, "The words are yours, I AM." Luke's auditors fill in the third person, "And HE IS." The court says, "Why call more witnesses? His own mouth condemns him."

How the admission to being "the Son of God" could be considered a capital offense has been subject to much debate. The fact is that in Luke's Gospel Jesus ordinarily refers to himself as the Son of humanity, a description that includes reference to his fragile human existence. In Luke's story the leaders know what the general public knows. That this person, who is a threat to the security of the nation (see 23:2), should dare to call himself the Son of God in the sense of exercising divine power, is unbearable. He poses a danger to Jerusalem and to Rome.

Whatever the precise exchange may have been, Luke's account retains its intellectual as well as literary integrity. Luke projects his awareness of the fact that preconceptions of guilt have often introduced into criminal proceedings assumptions concerning the meaning of words that in other contexts would send up less volatile signals. In any case, a yes-or-no situation is no fertile soil for sustained intelligible rhetoric and Luke shows that he has a sensitive nose for the scent of history by giving the weight of rhetorical impact to the expression *egō eimi*, "I am." This is the fatal innoculation of the term "Son of God." Ordinarily, the term might be applied to any Israelite. But Luke knows that the chief priest could bring other associations to the use of this expression.

For "I am" is also a claim appropriate to Yahweh (Exod. 3:14; Isa. 43:10; 46:4; 48:12; 51:12; 52:6). "I am, there is no other!" exclaimed Yahweh (45:18). Isaiah took Babylon to task for arrogantly asserting for itself, "I am, there is no other," and confronted it with the prospect of a city full of widows (47:8).

Against such biblical background Luke's record of Jesus' self-incrimination is credible. So intimately is Jesus linked with the heavenly will and purpose that his mind and thought merge with that of his Parent. Far from being a revolutionary who is subversive to Yahweh's interests, Jesus recognized Yahweh to be the ultimate arbiter of righteousness (Luke 18:19). Ironically, the earlier experience of Yahweh with Israel (Isaiah 48, esp. v. 18) becomes the experience of Jesus with the city for which he had hoped to be its peace (Luke 19:42). Some of Luke's public could be presumed to be familiar with Isaiah's contents (Acts 8:32–33; 17:10–12), and while hearing the account of Jesus' condemnation for saying "I am" they would fill in between the lines: "Not Jesus, but Jerusalem picked up the rhetoric of Babylon, and it was she who lost her children, as our Lord foretold" (see Luke 19:44 and Acts 28:26–27).

Appeal to the Scriptures—Only Jesus Qualifies

Concomitant with Luke's presentation of Jesus' commitment to the divine will is the emphasis he places on the correspondence of important moments in Jesus' life and death with the Scriptures. The passages of most interest for our study of the manner in which Luke shows how the Son-of-David category is transcended by a proper view of Jesus' divine Sonship include Psalms 2, 15 (16) and 109 (110), and Isaianic passages including selected "Servant" songs. From the interplay of his use of these passages and from his editorial modification of synoptic parallels we are able to determine how he anticipated a strengthening of his christological case through such appeal to the Scriptures. Through Psalms 2 and 109 (110), Luke could deal with the notion that Jesus lacked messianic credentials because of his failure to fulfill all prophetic Davidic expectations. Crucial to his argument is the factor of Jesus' resurrection and his subsequent ascension. Hence, Peter says in Acts 2:34 that David did not ascend into heaven. In fact, David himself said: "The Lord said to my Lord, 'Sit down at my right hand, until I make a footrest out of your enemies' " (Ps. 109 [110]:1). Since it is Jesus whom God raised from the dead and exalted to heaven, argues Peter (Acts 2:32–33), it is evident that only Jesus qualifies for the action described by David in this psalm.

In Luke 20:42–44 we find the same citation which the evangelist had taken from his source (Mark 12:36). Luke had previously moved Mark 12:28–34, which appeared to him an intrusive discussion, to Luke 10:25–28. This shift enabled him to close the gap between the discussion about the resurrection

(20:27–40) and the question of Jesus' Davidic credentials (vv. 41–47), because for Luke this question revolved around the resurrection of Jesus. Luke did not suggest that Jesus' Davidic association was inconsequential, but that Jesus' divine Sonship takes precedence over any evaluations made about him in the light of preconceived notions about the outcome of prophecy associated with the name of David or his alleged heirs. In short, nonfulfillment of national hopes for glory and deliverance from gentile enemies does not invalidate Jesus' credentials.

Son of God from Birth to Resurrection
According to the Scriptures

I have already observed that Psalm 2 provided Luke with his two principal christological terms, "Christ" and "Lord" (v. 2). This psalm also contains the words: "You are my son; today I became your father" (v. 7). This verse is used to reinforce Paul's proclamation of the resurrection of Jesus (Acts 13:33). The resurrection of Jesus, being a restoration to life, is a fresh birthday experience.

Of special interest is the fact that the citation from Psalm 2 duplicates an earlier one in Luke 3:22, which deletes the words "today I became your father" but includes words not found in Psalm 2: "in you I delight." The latter expression is quite probably derived from Isa. 42:1. Both this verse and Luke 3:21–22 speak of the Lord's chosen one who is endowed with the Spirit. Later on, Luke 4:18 not only reflects Isa. 58:6 and 61:1–2, but also 42:6.

It is apparent, then, that Luke has used Psalm 2 to document two phases of Sonship for Jesus: one at his birth announced to the shepherds and subsequently confirmed at his baptism, and the other through his resurrection. Psalm 15 (16):8–11, cited in Acts 2:25–28, lends further support to Luke's line of interpretation. Israel's rejection of Jesus does not nullify his messianic credentials. On the contrary, in a beneficent gesture of mercy God mercifully gives the Messiah a second time to Israel and through the apostolic mission to the world. The Sonship of Jesus is thus viewed as a continuing recognition by his heavenly Parent of an identity only apparently disrupted by the crucifixion. For even at the height of what seemed to be complete disaster for him, instead of crying out as a derelict (Mark 15:34) Jesus triumphantly returned his *pneuma*, his Spirit, to the Father for safe deposit (Luke 23:46). His death is real, but there is no hiatus in his Sonship with the Father. God's anointing "takes" permanently.

In line with such editorial maneuver is his presentation of the appeal to the Scriptures recorded in Mark 14:21 and Matt. 26:24. Having already in Luke 18:31 affirmed scriptural testimony concerning the Son of humanity, at 22:22 he substitutes the word *horizō* ("determine"), which reflects more explicitly his view of divine direction in human affairs and at the same time interprets his use of scriptural testimony. The Scriptures are for Luke a written expression of divine control of history. It is his alternative to the Greco-Roman doctrine of fortune (*tychē*). In effect, the use of the term here in 22:22 anticipates the theological amplification in Acts 2:23, where the same term appears in connection with the citation of Psalm 15 (16):8–11. Similarly, Acts 10:42 and 43 relate divine determination to prophetic anticipation. Acts 17:26, 31 expresses the thought in general terms—God is in charge of the welfare of the nations and has "fixed a day on which the world will be judged . . . by one whom God has appointed."

Luke was apparently satisfied that he had firmly established the credentials of Jesus through his disposition of the tradition up to the last breath of Jesus (Luke 23:46). Hence it was less important for him to repeat Mark's affirmation of Jesus' divine Sonship (Mark 15:39), expressed through the centurion, than to accent the dynamic aspect of Jesus' Sonship, his complete conformity with the Father's purpose. Therefore Luke records the centurion as saying, "Truly this man was upright" (*dikaios*, 23:47). This verdict is in keeping with the contrast Luke builds up in the passion narrative between Jesus' innocence and the guilt especially of the religious establishment. The contrast in turn serves as the background for the early apostolic proclamation on this particular point, which is most articulately expressed in Acts 3:14, a passage that echoes both Luke 1:35 and 23:47. Son of David *or* Son of God? Luke's answer: Obedient Son of God *and* David's heir—the Just One.

To a Greco-Roman public, the centurion's verdict ("innocent," "upright") meant that Jesus was declared a person of exceptional merit by a Roman representative. Piety and righteousness were the standard marks of such distinguished people. After detailing in his *Res Gestae* the benefits he had conferred on Rome, Caesar Augustus proudly recalled that the Roman people had awarded him a gold shield with this inscription: "A man of exceptional merit and forebearance, of upright (*iustitia*) and reverent character." Jesus had displayed all of that during his trial, and no one was more pious than he in the hour of death (23:46). With consummate economy Luke permits the centurion to pronounce the second component of Greco-Romans' claim to honor. And Luke's publics hear it in full: "Truly a man of exceptional merit, a benefactor, known for his piety and uprightness."

Apocalyptic Credentials of Jesus— Elijah, Son of Humanity

Next to the problem of Jesus' Davidic credentials or apparent lack of them, the question of the relation between Jesus and his future role as Son of humanity required close attention by Luke. He had to take account also of the role played by Elijah in apocalyptic tradition.

Discussion of all respects of traditions relating to the term "Son of humanity" is not vital to this brief study. From a linguistic perspective much of the discussion concerning the alleged barbarity of the Greek expression is gratuitous. Its grammatical contours (*ho huios tou anthrōpou*, the son of the human being) are not unique in biblical Greek. John 17:12 and 2 Thess. 2:3, for instance, have the phrase "the son of perdition" (*ho huios tēs apoleias*, the son of the perdition), and the LXX contains the plural formulation *hoi huioi tōn anthrōpōn* (the sons of the human beings). The vocative form (*huie anthrōpou*), as used time and again in Ezekiel, naturally appears without articles because of the definite force inherent in the vocative, but the singular form of the second component may well account for the singular form in the corresponding component of the expression used by Jesus. The use of the singular, then, in reference to Jesus stresses his unique affiliation with humanity in the same way that the term *ho huios tou theou* emphasizes his unique affiliation with God.

It is not fashionable to associate the term "Son of humanity" as used by Jesus with Ezekiel's use, but the parable-explanation complex used in Mark 4 is taken over by Luke and may well reflect early association of Jesus with the prophet Ezekiel (see Ezek. 17:12–24; 24:6–14). As did the prophet Ezekiel (3:4–11), Jesus also encounters resistance from his own people. Because of his interest in Jesus' association with those who have either little status in the religious life of Israel or because of personal disabilities or character are disbarred from normal social intercourse, Luke would find the term "Son of humanity" additionally useful to thread the fabric of that side of his story. The fact of Jesus' sociability is well established through Luke's numerous references to banquet scenes. Greco-Roman auditors would be especially quick to note in his quaint phrase the pandemic thrust of the Great Benefactor.

In general, then, the use of the appellation by Luke's Jesus refers to his total identification with the fragile, mortal lot of humanity, and to such an extent that he pays the ultimate fee in acceptance of his assignment as an Israelite dedicated to God's purposes. Hence Luke's adoption of the numerous passion predictions. The fact that the term is used in some of these and other passages that speak of victory does not negate the preceding interpretation. The point is that it is the same Jesus, the fragile sufferer, who ultimately wins and comes as deliverer and judge (Acts 1:11). God sticks with Jesus even after the crucifixion!

It now remains to explore the main lines of Luke's thought and interpret their interrelationships, with the inquiry confined to Luke's incorporation and editorial modification especially of the material extant in Mark and parallel non-Markan portions in Matthew, itemized as Q.

Mark's Solution

Whatever the route may have been whereby the "Son of humanity" was viewed in some circles as an apocalyptic figure, Mark strongly affirms, as does the tradition in

Q, the personal unity of Jesus and the Son of humanity. Mark also brought sayings, not found in Q, about the necessity of the suffering that befalls the Son of humanity (Mark 8:31; 9:31; 10:33).

Furthermore, Mark was anxious to show that the person of Jesus is not to be separated from the one "whom they will see . . . coming in clouds with great power and glory" (Mark 13:26). The apocalyptic expectations, now linked with Jesus, would not be disappointed. Immediately after his report of the transfiguration of Jesus, and the reference to the Son of humanity's resurrection (Mark 9:2–9), Mark introduced a dialogue between the disciples and Jesus concerning the function of Elijah in the end time. According to Jesus' reply, Elijah had already made his appearance. Mark's audience knows that John the Baptist is meant, for in the very first chapter (1:6) he had been depicted as the revered prophet. Now the point is that John the Baptist, like Elijah of old, had met his Ahab and Jezebel (see Mark 6:14–29), and John the Baptist's death becomes the model for Jesus' own fate. In any event, there is no other forerunner for the apocalyptic deliverer. That deliverer is Jesus, and the forerunner has come, says Mark, in the person of John the Baptist, alias Elijah. Ergo, the end of the end time is imminent.

Luke's Critique of John as Elijah

Together with Mark, Luke is very sympathetic to the tradition that equates Jesus and the Son of humanity, but in his judgment Mark's type of proclamation did not adequately meet the needs of Christian communities that were being disturbed either by forecasters of the apocalyptic events that terminate the world's existence, or by others who variously questioned the credentials of Jesus, the promise of his return, and his identity as Son of humanity in terms of some application of Dan. 7:13. Luke had grave doubts about the wisdom of defending one apocalyptic sector, the Son of humanity traditions, against misunderstanding by bringing in troops from another that would be equally vulnerable, the Elijah tradition. To head off the threat, Luke endeavored to move the christological question to a point where Jesus' messianic credentials would not be at the mercy of the vicissitudes of history or subject to curious speculation.

Jesus Independent of John

Instead of deleting references to John the Baptist, Luke fills his opening chapters with stories about him, but in such a way that John is no longer an apocalyptic figure, but a contemporary of Jesus with only a six-month lead (1:36), and considerably inferior to Jesus in status and endowment. Whatever adulation is heaped on him is done in the rhetorical spirit of the East, which will pour praises on a mother in order indirectly to express admiration for a brilliant offspring (see, e.g., Luke 11:27). The traditional association of John with Elijah is maintained (1:17) but in such a way that John is *not* made a forerunner of Jesus but of "the Lord their God." He is to go before "him" (this demonstrative points to the preceding reference to God), and he is to do this in the "spirit and power of Elijah." That is, he is to be a great prophet. But, as Luke is quick to point out in the corresponding annunciation, Jesus' experience of spirit and power is far superior, for he enters the world as a result of the Holy Spirit's action. Luke interprets this as "power of the highest" (1:35). Therefore, in keeping with the theology of the annunciation, Luke says in a later description of Jesus' baptism, that God anointed him with "the Holy Spirit and with power" (Acts 10:38).

Since John is not a messenger who in his person validates the identity of Jesus, Luke shifts Mark 1:2—which is derived from Exod. 23:20 and Mal. 3:1—to Luke 7:27. With the passage as he has it in 3:4–6, Luke achieves the following:

1. He eliminates Mark's apocalyptic association of John with Elijah from his own presentation of John's public ministry.

2. He clarifies the quotation as one derived wholly from Isaiah, which is Luke's favorite source next to the Psalms.

3. Through the clear echo of Simeon's reference to God's salvation (2:30) in the concluding clause, "all flesh shall see God's salvation" (3:6), Luke historicizes what would be traditionally taken as apocalyptic anticipation. God's salvation comes, not in end-time special effects, but in the person of Jesus, first witnessed by a Jew named Simeon, and then proclaimed to all the world through the apostolic mission recorded in Acts.

4. Repentance, a favorite theme of Luke's, comes to expression in the figurative language of Isaiah. Acts 13:10 will further clarify how Luke understands this prophetic passage.

Concerning Luke's shift of Mark 1:2 to Luke 7:27, it is to be observed that the term rendered "prepare" in 7:27 is used only once elsewhere in Luke's work, namely at 1:17, where it is the people who are prepared for the Lord God. Because Luke wished to separate John from Elijah, 1:17 does not use the Greek word "restore" which appears in Mark 9:12 and is derived from Mal. 3:23 [4:6]. Through the quotation in 7:27 Luke affirmed that John the Baptist functioned as a leader of God's people and prepared the way before the people (see Exod. 23:20, especially in its LXX form). That Luke understood the passage in this way is also seen from his introduction (7:29–30) to a tradition from Q. Similarly Acts 13:24 carefully states not that John was a forerunner in terms of whom the messianic credentials of Jesus could be verified but one who functioned as herald and proclaimed repentance "before the face of his (Jesus') entrance," as Luke semitically phrases it. Thus John serves within Luke's narrative as a model for apostolic preachers of all time who through their preaching have the stage set by God for the reception of forgiveness in connection with the supreme expression of divine beneficence, Jesus Christ.

Not John but Jesus is Elijah

Because of his emphasis on Jesus' total commitment to God's purpose, Luke omitted Mark's reference (15:34) to a cry of dereliction. A further factor influencing this editorial decision was Mark's association of the cry with a reference to Elijah (Mark 15:35). Luke not only dissociates John from Elijah but moves in the positive direction of letting Jesus' ministry overlap in some respects that of Elijah-Elisha. Thus Jesus explicitly ministers to "outsiders" in the manner of Elijah and his immediate successor (4:25–27). Luke 7:11–17 would evoke reminiscences of 1 Kings 17 and 2 Kings 4 in some of Luke's public. The story of the grateful leper (Luke 17:12–19) may well articulate memories of the cure of Naaman (2 Kings 4). And, like Elijah (see 2 Kings 2 and Jesus ben Sirach 48:9), Jesus makes an ascension (9:51; Acts 1:2, 11, 22), while endowing his Elisha-like successor, the apostolic community, with a rich measure of his Spirit. But that community is not to specialize in one aspect of Elijah's ministry—apocalyptic fire. Copyists of 9:54 were evidently aware of Luke's Jesus-Elijah-typology, for they inserted the phrase "just as Elijah did" after the disciples' request for incendiary weapons to be used against Samaria. For their lapse into vengeful attitudes the disciples are roundly rebuked and hustled to another town.

By thus linking Elijah loosely with Jesus, Luke steers attention away from intermediary apocalyptic figures or apocalyptic events in terms of whom the Messiah's presence or credentials are to be evaluated. Instead, the messianic and apocalyptic hopes are merged in one person—Jesus, who is the Son of God on assignment to restore all things (Acts 3:21). That restoration is in progress through the apostolic mission which does its work under the authority of the Spirit in the name of Jesus. And Greco-Roman auditors would note that *apokatastasis* (restoration) was the beneficent work of such heads of state as Ptolemy V, who is celebrated on the Rosetta Stone, and Nero.[2]

Luke's Critique of Son of Humanity Tradition

By rerouting Mark's use of apocalyptic Elijah-typology Luke was able to bring the tradition relating to the Son of humanity into sharper focus. Again, his omissions, additions, and alterations in respect to the use of this term suggest the unity of his conception.

Luke's treatment of Mark's recital *after the transfiguration* (Mark 9:9–13) is instructive. In his record (Luke 9:28–36), Luke is anxious to cite as the next episode after the transfiguration Mark's story about an exorcism (Luke 9:37–43 = Mark 9:14–29). Therefore the episode takes place "after their descent from the mountain" (Luke 9:37). Luke deletes the conversation which Mark says took place on the way down. He then changes a command to silence into a statement of reaction to "what they had seen," with the result that the following scene becomes an integral episode of the transfiguration recital rather than a postlude. Through this verbal alteration and shift Luke is also able to dissociate the explicit term "Son of humanity" from the transfiguration episode, capitalize on the heavenly voice that reaffirms the divine Sonship of Jesus, and focus attention on "what they had seen" as the main factor and corollary of the permanent glory that Jesus possesses after his suffering (24:26). In this way Luke's transfiguration recital, integrated as it is in his realized christological apocalyptic, discourages curious speculation and directs stronger attention to the death of Jesus. To further achieve this latter objective, Luke adds the information not found in the other synoptists, namely, that Moses and Elijah (in different sequence from Mark 9:4!) spoke about the exodus Jesus would accomplish in Jerusalem (Luke 9:31). In Luke's transfiguration narrative the suffering and the subsequent glory are associated, and Jesus stands together with Moses and Elijah in an anticipation of the gesture noted in Acts 7:56.

Within the same conceptual framework lies the concluding sentence of Luke's record of the exorcism: "And he gave him back to his father, and they all were astounded at the majesty of God" (v. 43). This is terminology appropriate to special divine intervention. With this sentence, unique in the synoptic tradition, Luke achieves three objectives. First, having put the stories of the transfiguration and the exorcism back to back, without the staccato effect injected by Mark 9:9–10, Luke shows that the apocalyptic moment is not to be sought in traditional end-time fireworks, but is already present in the work and message of Jesus. Second, with the phrase "he gave him back to his father," Luke echoes an earlier incident, the story of the raising of the youth at Nain (7:11–17), which similarly terminates with a reminiscence of accounts in 1 Kings 17:23 (Elijah) and 2 Kings 4:36 (Elisha). Third, the word "majesty" is referred specifically to God. This is in keeping with Luke's view of God's providential generosity, now displayed in connection with Jesus' ministry. Three disciples saw the glory of Jesus, but a "great crowd" (9:37) now experiences the majesty of God. But what Jesus did here was only part of the beginning. The apostolic church sees and hears the ongoing revelation of the majesty of God. In this manner Luke employed the gospel genre in the interests of christologized apocalyptic, which relieves Christians of the necessity to speculate about the signs of the times.

Other Editorializing on
Son-of-Humanity Tradition

Although the question of Luke's use of Mark's passion narrative is beset with difficulties, it is nevertheless a fact that Luke does not verbatim record Mark 14:41. But his rhetorical skill is displayed in the manner whereby he substantially retains the import of the tradition found in Mark. The "hour" is specifically described and more dramatically articulated at Luke 22:53 as a demonically permeated moment, with mention of the participants who were earlier cited in a specific passion prediction (9:22). The content of Mark's reference to the betrayal of the Son of humanity (Mark 14:41) is rephrased at a later point in Luke's recital (22:22) so as to give even more dramatic impact to Judas' betrayal. With a kiss of friendship (v. 48) he turns in the one who is frail humanity personified, yet the judge of all humanity (21:27; Acts 17:31).

Luke 22:24–27 displays a shift of Mark 10:41–45 into the passion narrative, but with omission of Mark's ransom motif and its accompanying reference to the Son of humanity, who is already mentioned in Luke 22:22 (= Mark 14:21). For Luke it is God who gives Jesus as a supreme benefaction to the world. Hence there is no need to speak of a ransom. Furthermore, Jesus, Lord of the people of God, is permanently in their midst in the paradoxical position of "servant" by virtue of his obedience to the Father, who "covenants" with him a kingdom (22:28–29) that is realized through the cross and resurrection (see Acts 2:36).

Besides omissions, Luke makes a number of alterations in Mark's Son-of-humanity statements that he retains. A simple shift of the demonstrative "his" in 9:26 makes Jesus independent possessor of, not merely participant in, the glory attributed in Mark 8:38 to the Father. At 9:44 Luke omits the reference made by Mark (9:31) to Jesus' resurrection, for Luke aims to emphasize the suffering, which contrasts with the realized apocalyptic of the two preceding recitals, and thus focuses attention on the content of what the disciples were to hear (9:35–36).

In connection with Jesus' reply to the Sanhedrin, Luke 22:69 contains significant changes relative to Mark 14:62. First, he holds to the tradition based on Psalm 109 (110):1 (see Luke 20:42; Acts 2:34) that Jesus assumed his position at the right hand of God in connection with his resurrection, a tradition that surfaces also in Luke 22:29–30; therefore he emphasizes that the session takes place "from now on," thus anticipating the interpretation expressed in 24:26. Second, in place of "you shall see," which for Mark is patently futuristic apocalyptic, Luke reads "the Son of humanity will be. . . ." Thereby the credentials of Jesus as Son of humanity are again, in harmony with a passage like 17:20-25, taken out of the realm of curious speculation. Third, the Son of humanity does not "come" with the clouds, as he does in Mark. Luke had earlier discussed (7:18-23) the question of "the coming one" and affirmed that the Son of humanity "had come" (7:34, perfect tense, instead of aorist as used in Matt. 11:19). In accordance with Luke's two-phase apocalyptic view, the Son of humanity will come at the end of the end time (Acts 1:11). In the meantime he sits at the right hand of God, in charge of the apostolic mission.

Unique References to Son of Humanity in Luke

Luke's numerous references to Son of humanity not found in Mark and Matthew point further to his interest in the apocalyptic problem. His attention to the tradition that underlies 17:22, about "seeing" one of the days of the Son of man, stems from a desire to reconcile a promise, such as that expressed in 9:27, with the disappointment engendered by the nonarrival of apocalyptic deliverance. The kingdom of God, Luke teaches, is not to be confused with an apocalyptic moment, for the kingdom of God is "present among you" (17:21), namely in the activity of Jesus (see 10:9). But the kingdom comes also in a second phase, that is, as the end of all history, with a suddenness (not imminence) that none can calculate (17:24). The question is, will the Son of humanity find faith anywhere? (18:8). Put that way, Luke's auditor is prompted to reply, "Then my troubles and disasters are no indication that Jesus' apocalyptic credentials are out of order."

Rather than emphasize Jesus' judicial role as the Son of humanity, Luke 19:10 presents him on the scene in search of the lost. This approach is again in keeping with Luke's theme of the function of Jesus as the ultimate expression of God's beneficence.

An elegant contrast helps to structure the material around the reference to the Son of humanity in 6:22. Ironically, those who expel Christians from their community because of their commitment to Jesus, the Son of humanity—at 21:12 Jesus says, "for the sake of my name"—will find the objects of their persecution enjoying the rewards for faithful witness. The response of rejoicing (6:23) anticipates in a way the gleeful resistance to the chief priests and elders that was displayed by the friends of Peter and John after the release of the two apostles (Acts 4:23-31). The passage betrays Luke's editorial pen, for it bears the synthetic marks of his realized apocalyptic.

Together with Matthew (see Matt. 10:32-33 and 12:31-32), Luke 12:8-10 endeavors to adapt to fresh circumstances a dominical saying dominant in the area where Q was popular. Whereas Matthew reduces Son of humanity to "I" in the phrase "I also will intervene before my Father in heaven," Luke reads, "also the Son of humanity will intervene before God's angels." It is not easy to decide which evangelist does the greater editorial work relative to Q within these specific verses, but it is certain that Luke is responsible for bringing the thought expressed in 12:10 into juxtaposition with vv. 8–9. Quite evidently Peter himself would have fallen under the injunction of v. 9, for he had denied Jesus (22:57). Therefore v. 10 offers Luke's "corrective" to what must have appeared an intolerable saying. It is not a word spoken against the Son of humanity, but one uttered against the Holy Spirit that will not be forgiven. Luke thereby renders more meaningful his perspective on the second chance that is offered in the post-Pentecost proclamation. One must not trifle with divine beneficence. At the same time the evangelist sharpens his instruction on hardness of heart (8:10; 24:25–31). In all this a Western mind might infer a contradiction. But ears that were accustomed to the kind of dissonance expressed in popular logic, such as Prov. 26:4, 5, would hear a piece of wisdom that corresponded to the realities and demands of human experience.

Luke 21:36 terminates an apocalyptic discourse with the admonition to be watchful, so as to be able to "stand before the Son of humanity." Whereas popular apocalyptic appealed to people because it promised deliverance and simultaneously encouraged speculation about the end, thereby creating confusion among God's people, Luke emphasized that it is more important to ask whether one is prepared to stand in the presence of the Son of humanity. For such the end will be no problem. And, as his ministry attests, Jesus is no sponsor of a select class or national group.

At 22:48 Luke adds a conversational detail to the scene of Judas' betrayal: "Is it with a kiss that you betray the Son of humanity?" Luke lays to rest forever any question about the identity of the Son of humanity. And through the word "betray" he gives a sharp focus to the meaning of 9:44 and 18:32.

The last reference to the Son of humanity in Luke's Gospel appears at 24:7, in a context reminiscent of the transfiguration narrative and sequel (9:28–45). Just as the transfiguration, with its satellite narrative of an exorcism (9:37–43), was preceded (v. 22) and followed (v. 44) by references to Jesus' fate in Jerusalem, so the resurrection account (24:1–6) follows the passion recital and leads into a reference to the passion-resurrection script that Jesus followed (v. 7). The women at the tomb now recall what Jesus had said (cf. 9:22). Thus Luke affirms the death and resurrection of Jesus as a climactic apocalyptic phase still in progress. Henceforth, except for one reference in Acts 7:56, Luke will make no more mention of the Son of humanity. Son of David, Son of God, and Son of humanity will all give way to Christ and Lord.

Christ and Lord

Luke's favorite titles for Jesus are *Christos* (Anointed One = Messiah, in Hebrew) and *Kyrios* (Lord). By embedding them in the birth narrative (2:11) and in the apostolic preaching (Acts 2:36) Luke encourages no doubt regarding their importance.

Christ—The Anointed One

To help eliminate any suggestion of an adoptive ceremony later at the Jordan (Luke 3:22), Luke emphasizes that Simeon cradles the Lord's Christ in his arms (2:26-28), and this one, the Christ, is identified as God's salvation (v. 30). In denominating him so, Luke calls for the discarding of all blueprints that do not match the divine purpose.

As John the Baptist asserted of Jesus when asked whether he himself was the Anointed One (3:15-16), being the Christ means to be in possession of anointing power, for the Christ "will baptize with the Holy Spirit and fire." What was affirmed to Mary in the annunciation (1:35) and reaffirmed at the baptism (3:22) is self-confirmed by Jesus at Nazareth after citation from the Scriptures (4:21). For the benefit especially of his Greco-Roman auditors Luke thus establishes that the terms "Son of God" and "Christ" are equivalents in the case of Jesus. Once this has been done, they will be able to follow a story line that necessarily includes matters of intense interest to those of Jewish ancestry.

The words ascribed to Isaiah (3:18-19) are taken from various parts of the book and presented with some editorial freedom in the sequence Isa. 61:1; 58:6; 61:2. But the verb in 4:18, "anointed," is in its Greek form *echrisen* (equivalent to making a verb out of the title Christ) the primary point of the christological focus. Jesus, who received his messianic credentials directly through the Spirit, is preeminently a proclaimer to the poor. Through such proclamation the "acceptable year of Yahweh" becomes reality. This last term would have conveyed apocalyptic overtones to some of Luke's public. In keeping with his endeavor to discourage speculation about apocalyptic developments, Luke shows that the apocalyptic moment takes place as the first of two phases in the Spirit-filled ministry of Jesus.

The Anointed One as Apocalyptic
Counselor and Denouncer

If proclamation to the poor means that the apocalyptic moment is now, it is not surprising that in the opening beatitude of the Sermon on the Plain Jesus should affirm the present reality of the kingdom for the benefit of the poor (6:20), that is, for those who would be considered least likely to receive the messianic benefactions. In scenes reminiscent of this sermon, the widow at Nain would have no reason to weep any longer (7:13) and over five thousand people would have their hunger satisfied (9:12-17). Both experiences suggest the fullness of blessing that awaits the believing community in the second phase of the kingdom when Jesus will come from heaven (cf. Acts 8:21).

For this "consolation of Israel" (equivalent to the messianic time) Simeon had waited and he saw it (2:25-26). But woe to the "rich." Precisely because they already have their "consolation" (6:24), they get none. Instead they hear a lamentation. What Luke has in mind in all this can be partly determined from his story of the rich man and Lazarus (16:19–31) and the dialogue of Jesus with the rich ruler and the disciples (18:18–30). The man of luxury goes to perdition with the liturgy on his lips, and Lazarus is "now comforted" (16:25). The rich ruler is told to sell all he has and divide it among the poor, something Christians after Pentecost took seriously, to judge from Peter's reminder addressed to Jesus (Luke 18:28) and the voluntary sharing that took place after Pentecost (Acts 2:44–45). The answer in Luke 18:29–30 to Peter's question reflects the actual situation in the course of the apostolic mission, and the conjunction of "this time" and "the age to come" is with its expression of two-phase apocalyptic in harmonious continuity with the opening sentence of the Sermon on the Plain.

The Great Omission

In the light of our earlier analyses and the line of thought expressed in 4:18 and 6:20–49, it is now possible to examine the rhetorical rationale behind Luke's "great omission" of Mark 6:45—8:26.

Mark's narrative (6:45—8:26) is thematically coherent in its larger context, but Luke's interests were different, and much of the material contained in Mark's account either partially duplicated traditions used by Luke or were incompatible with his thematic interests. The question of Elijah's role in the verification of Jesus' messianic credentials was of prime interest to Luke. Therefore he seized first on the transparent unity afforded by the reminiscences of Elijah that surfaced in Mark 6—8. Mark's first feeding narrative (Mark 6:31–44; Luke 9:10–17) not only accommodated well the promise in Luke 6:21, but tied into Luke's effort to conjoin the ministries of Elijah and Jesus, in contrast to Mark's more consistent link of Elijah and John the Baptist. Elisha's activity recorded in 2 Kings 4 would not be lost on Luke's public once they heard or read his succeeding references to Elijah. Artistically, the pericope comprising 9:18–27, with its reference especially to John the Baptist and Elijah (v. 19), is now well motivated, and a link is forged with the pericope concerning Herod's perplexity. (9:7–9).

There might appear to be an element of hazard in Luke's method of refuting interpretation of John's ministry as the work of a latter-day Elijah who ushers in the great day of Yahweh. By connecting Elijah with Jesus Luke seems to run the risk of defeating one of his primary objectives, namely, to show that Jesus is in a class by himself (Acts 4:12), and that all the prophets attest him (Luke 24:44). But Luke's technique of using traditions as hermeneutical stepping-stones to the understanding of God's larger purpose in Jesus protects his work from such rhetorical broken circuits. Just as he had corrected misdirection in use of the Davidic category, so he rerouted the contributions of the Elijah-Elisha traditions in such a way that the unique significance of Jesus could be better apprehended.

Not without point, therefore, does Luke introduce into Jesus' question an alteration of "men" to "the crowds" (9:18). Popular messianism is to be distinguished from what Luke considers orthodox messianism. The answer of the disciples in v. 19 suggests that a distinction between the ministries of John the Baptist and Elijah, as well as association of the ministry of Jesus with that of Elijah were available to Luke in a form that suffered from insufficient reflection. At the same time, Luke's addition of the verb "has risen" in 9:19 suggests that he was verbalizing even more pointedly than his source a strong tendency within the community to interpret Jesus in terms of a revived figure from the past (see, e.g., 16:31) and thus somehow adapt faith in him to presuppositions concerning apocalyptic hopes. The hope of a resurrection of the righteous, and in the very near future, was linked with such views. Therefore Luke rephrases Mark's Petrine answer, "You are the Anointed One" (Mark 8:29), with the simple phrase "the Christ of God" (Luke 9:20). The addition "of God" signals the words in 2:26, which state that Simeon was not to die until he had seen "the Christ of Yahweh." God, and God alone, makes Jesus Lord and Messiah.

Jesus is not "prophet redivivus"; he is the end-time salvation, already seen by Simeon. Since the problem faced by Luke is one of apocalyptic misunderstanding, he brings into immediate juxtaposition the passion prediction about the Son of humanity (9:22). Thus the apocalyptic hope is taken seriously, but joined immediately with the death of Jesus. *After his death* he would rise. Jesus does not make his appearance as a revivified prophet, but he will rise after his death has taken place. The resurrection of Jesus' followers will be part of the second apocalyptic phase, when Jesus, the Son of humanity who suffered (9:22), returns as the Christ who possesses glory by virtue of the fulfillment of his assigned task (see 24:26) and returns in that same glory (9:26; cf. Acts 1:11).

Christ of God—The Elect One

Back-to-back with 9:18-27 is Luke's rendition of the transfiguration. Of importance here is the wording of the divine voice: "This is my Son, the elect one; listen to him" (9:35). The main clues to Luke's choice of diction here are given in 23:35, which bears the stamp of thoroughgoing editorial work. First, the formal character of the additional words "of God" expresses Luke's intention to link 23:35-38 with the infancy narrative (2:26) and the story of Peter's confession (9:20). Second, the adjective "elect" is applied to Jesus only in 23:35 in all of Luke's writing, and the cognate verb is similarly used of Jesus only in the transfiguration recital (9:35). Third, the conditional form is indicative of Luke's intention to link this mockery as a temptation akin to the type expressed in 4:1-13. The common factor in all of this editorializing is Luke's thematic reflection on the Sonship of Jesus.

As the Son of God, Jesus had encountered Satan, who awaited a "convenient time" (4:11). That time had come at the Passover Feast (22:3). But Luke also had put the story of Jesus' experience at Nazareth back to back with the temptation narrative. Through the citations from Isaiah (61:1-2; 58:6) he gave further expression to a cardinal theme, Jesus, the Servant of the Lord, anointed by the Spirit (see below, chap. 6). According to Isa. 42:1, God would accept Jacob as child (*pais*), and elect Israel would be endowed with the divine spirit. Thus equipped, Israel was to bear justice to the nations (see also Isa. 44:1-5). Jesus is Jacob, God's Son; he is Israel personified, and as "one who slaves for many" he, the Righteous One, will be put in the right by the Lord (Isa. 53:11, LXX). It is a truism that Luke shapes his passion narrative in such a way that the innocence of Jesus finds confirmation in numerous ways. But it is especially significant that Luke, after reaffirming the Sonship of Jesus in the departing prayer (23:46), has the centurion pronounce the divine verdict, "Truly this man was righteous" (v. 47).

From all this it appears that Isaiah's description of the Servant as Son of God, elected and righteous, quite evidently hovered in Luke's mind as he edited the climactic stage of the passion account. But Psalm 2 was also clearly in his mind, for in Acts 4:27 he paraphrased Ps. 2:2 in order to describe the very hostility that Jesus encountered at Luke 23:35. Moreover, it is precisely Psalm 2 that contains the formulaic background for Luke's phrase, "the Christ of God." Acts 4:26 repeats verbatim the phrase, "against his Christ," which is equivalent to "the Christ of God." The same psalm goes on to quote Yahweh as saying: "You are my son" (v. 7).

With these data at hand we are now in a position to return to the interpretation of Luke's christological proclamation in 9:20 and 35. Both passages deal with Son of God, the first in association with Psalm 2, the second in association with the Isaianic Servant songs *and* Psalm 2. As Son of God, Jesus accepts the mission of the Suffering Servant, who is to be a light to the Gentiles (Isa. 42:6; Luke 2:32). As the Servant, he is God's Son, endowed with God's Spirit. Since the receipt of the Spirit, with God as mediator, is the dominant theological concern (see again Acts 10:38), the term "Christ" (thematically underlined in Luke 4:18) becomes next to "Lord" the main christological title, for it comprehends all the rest and helps put apocalyptic hope into proper perspective.

Other editorializing by Luke confirms the preceding analysis. At 4:41 Luke puts the term "Son of God" under the umbrella of "Anointed One." Then with Jesus' words in v. 43, "I must proclaim the kingdom of God, for I was sent for that purpose," he echoes the Christology pronounced in 4:18-21. In the presence of the Sanhedrin Jesus' claim to the title "Anointed One" is challenged, and by the ascending order of christological categories Luke shows how comprehensive the title is (22:67-70). With the recording of Jesus' affirmation, "I am," Luke eliminates all intermediaries, counterclaimants, or spectres of the future. The editing of 23:2 helps motivate Pilate's question about Jesus' claim to royalty (v. 3). The charge of subversiveness echoes the earlier tricky attempt to trap Jesus into saying something politically volatile (20:19-26). Jesus is the Lord's Anointed. As such he qualifies as a Davidian, and therefore as a king. As King-Messiah he will be identified in the charge that will be attached to his cross (23:38). The rationale of Luke's organization in 1:30-35 thus finds climactic expression.

At Luke 23:39, one of the two crucified criminals (*kakourgoi*) challenged Jesus with an echo of the temptations recorded in 4:1-8, and in a formulation which, like the one in 23:35, calls into question the divine equation in 2:11. In the dialogue of 23:40-43 the problem of Jesus' messianic credentials and of the apocalyptic anticipation of the kingdom of God is dramatically resolved. From external events no conclusions can be drawn respecting Jesus' credentials. The fact is that here is one who is innocent, (*dikaios*) and yet experiences the same fate as the guilty. This means that the answer to the question, how can God and man relate to one another, must come from God alone and cannot be derived from observation of external circumstances or events. Thrown back on faith in the goodness of God whose supreme benefaction is Jesus, the criminal next to Jesus displays repentance by rebuking the other malefactor, emphasizing that both of them are being "justly" (*dikaios*) punished and thereby indirectly anticipating the centurion's verdict. Then he addresses the central figure by name. The name Jesus gives the term Christ a personal dimension in which individuals can locate themselves meaningfully with reference to God, for Jesus is Savior. And when does the king come into his own? With his words to the criminal, Jesus gives expression to the heart of his kingdom claim: "Today you will be with me in paradise." What Jesus assured his disciples (22:29–30) he now promises to the criminal. The innocent one who counted many publicans and sinners among his friends (7:34) invites the guilty into the royal garden reserved for the righteous at the end of time. Executive pardon is a king's privilege, and this malefactor becomes the beneficiary of Jesus' first public act on the day of his coronation. Nor does a centurion, administrator of Roman justice, find fault with the proceeding (23:42).

With this one climactic stroke Luke delivered christological thought from all barnacles of special social privilege, nationalistic claim, cultic patronage, and speculative dreams. Via suffering the Anointed One entered into his glory (24:26), and all in accordance with the Scriptures (v. 44).

Kyrios (Lord, Master)

In contrast to the almost total absence of reference to the term Anointed One in the Q tradition, both Q and Luke's special source "L" make frequent use of the term *kyrios*. Almost half these references are in contexts which either explicitly or implicitly refer to master-slave relationships. According to numerous lines of OT tradition, the master-slave pair is used to describe relations between God and individuals, or between God and Israel. Jacob (Ezekiel 28:25), Moses (Malachi 3:24 [4:4]), and David (Ezekiel 34:23; 37:24) are all referred to as slaves, and in Jeremiah 26 (46):27–28 Jacob is called both a *doulos* ("slave") and a *pais* ("boy"). The term "slave" is applied in Isaiah 65:9 to chosen Israel. Opposed to those who despise Yahweh are God's faithful slaves in Israel, who will rejoice while the others lament (vv. 13–15; cf. Luke 6:20–26). Kings are told to slave for Yahweh, and with gladness (Psalm 2:11; see also Psalm 99 (100):2).

Use of the Master-Slave Pair in
Uniquely Lukan Tradition

Luke was quick to use the master-slave pair to describe the proper relationship between God or Jesus and the Christian community. Joel 3:2 (2:29), with its anticipation of an outpouring of the Spirit on God's slaves, both male and female, in the last days encouraged the use of this terminology. Mary, the slave of the *kyrios* (Luke 1:38), is the first recipient of the Holy Spirit (1:35), and her counterparts after Pentecost address Yahweh as their Master (Acts 2:18; 4:29). At Acts 16:17 a female medium correctly assesses Paul and his company as "slaves of the Most High God."

Luke's application of the term "slave" to a follower of Jesus is consistent with his view of God as Supreme Benefactor and of Jesus as the great expression of his benefactions. As do slaves of the systems of this world, Christians are to recognize that even after they have done all that was assigned them they are yet "useless slaves" (Luke 17:10). They are not to stand idly waiting to be congratulated for carrying out an assignment. If the Master chooses, he may compliment a slave, as at 19:17, but is under no obligation to do so. In such fashion Luke teaches the people of God to be free from enslavement to a moral bartering system.

In the parable of the waiting slaves (12:35–40) Peter appropriately asks, "Master, are you telling everyone this parable, or only us?" Luke goes on, "And the Master said. . . ." Then follows a parable that explains the other, and it quickly becomes clear that the leaders in the Christian community are to remember that in the absence of their Master, that is, before his return at the end of the end time, they are not to grasp ownership of the church and act as masters over others lower in the system. On the night of his betrayal, the Master reminded his disciples that the power structures of this world are in the business of lording it over others, but "it shall not be so among you," he admonished. Jesus reminded them that he was in their midst rendering service, that is, majoring in the business of bestowing benefits, not receiving them (22:24–27). Their business, then, is to major in beneficence, not in lordship.

Zacchaeus matched his address to Jesus, *kyrie* or "Master," with action appropriate to the title and his newly found relationship (19:8). Good slaves or imperial subjects move before they are asked. But besides that, Zacchaeus went far beyond the call of duty. He thus stands in marked contrast to those who merely exclaim, "Master! Master!" without doing what they are told (6:46; see also 7:7–8). The Great Benefactor had transformed a despised publican into a philanthropist.

Through his commanding word, the *Kyrios* of the church displays his presence. At 10:1 the mission of the seventy (seventy-two), reflective of the apostolic outreach to the world, begins with a specific reference to "The Master." Slaves were dispatched (*apostellō* is the Greek term) on varieties of errands. In the story of Mary and Martha (10:38–42), Jesus, "The Master" (vv. 39, 41), dispenses his word. Martha views him as a master who ought to distribute the work of the slaves properly. Why is she left to do all the serving? "Tell Mary to help me," she says. As in the case of the lawyer (10:25–37), Martha needs to gain a fresh perspective. The law says, "This do and you shall live" (v. 28). But to hear the word of the Master means to grow in understanding of the significance of his person and the depth of his commitment to the interests of humankind. For Jesus came not to be served but to serve (22:27). He is more than a distinguished rabbi for whom one must set a good table. He is himself the host.

As the Master who dispenses the word, Jesus interprets the significance of the sabbath (Luke 13:15). Heedless of the warning recited in 6:46, Peter promises to give the last measure of a slave's devotion (22:33), but after an almost lethal lapse of memory he remembers "the word of The Master" (v. 61). On the ready, the disciples say in response to Jesus' word about a sword, "Master, don't worry, we've already got some—here they are" (v. 38). Some estimate these disciples had of the battle that would be fought within the next few hours! Evidently Jesus' story about the king who underestimated his opponent had not sunk in (14:31).

Anyway, the quick service was more than Jesus could stand and he replied to this effect, "That should be enough to make us look like a band of outlaws!" But worse was yet to come. In the garden they ask, "Now, Master? Now?" Before he can intervene, one of them hacked off a piece of ear. On the spot Jesus did field surgery. Then he faced the enemy, and his words to them indicated that he, unlike the disciples, had not underestimated their forces and resources (22:53).

After his resurrection the word was out, "The Master has risen and he made an appearance to Simon" (24:34). This time the Master gives them orders to stay in Jerusalem until they get the power that will equip them for the world-wide task to be undertaken not in their names but his. And the fact that Jesus will return "in the same way" he was seen going into heaven (Acts 1:11) eliminates all rivals. From the time of Caesar Augustus to the end of time Jesus is the One Name.

CHAPTER SIX

SALVATION AND REPENTANCE

On the basis of the preceding chapters it is now evident that salvation is Luke's major theme. It is therefore necessary to explore it in detail, with special reference to the means of entry into the benefits of the New Age.

The preeminent experience of Israel is God's continuing mercy that spells ongoing salvation for everybody, everywhere (e.g., Luke 2:30–31). So recurrent are the expressions of this theme in the OT that it is almost impossible to open a page of the Psalms or Isaiah—Luke's favorite portions of the OT—without reading terms relating to it.

Of special interest are passages in Isaiah 39—66, in which the prophet associates salvation with such verbs as "make proclamation" (*euaggelizō*) and "console" (*parakaleō*). Isaiah begins his message with the divine exhortation, "Comfort, comfort my people" (Isa. 40:1). The comforter is then described in 40:9 as one who "makes proclamation" (the verb is *euaggelizomai;* the noun does not appear in the LXX version of Isaiah and is used only two times by Luke, in Acts 15:7; 20:24). The proclamation in Isa. 40:5 concerns God's salvation (*to sōtērion*), which is addressed, as in 52:7, to Jerusalem. In mercy God will relieve the oppressed of hunger and thirst (49:10). All who come from the land of their captivity "will proclaim" the Lord's salvation (60:6). So captivated is the prophet by the vision of Israel's future that he exclaims ecstatically the contents of his proclamation which spells consolation to the mourners (61:1–2), and, taking on the voice of Jerusalem, he rejoices in God's salvation (v. 10).

The Servant of the Lord

Being the recipient of salvation, Israel is taken into the service of God and is identified in Isaiah's prophecy as the Servant of the Lord. It is of course true that the identity of Isaiah's Servant fluctuates. At times he appears to be the prophet himself or some unique figure. But the corporate figure dominates.

As Israel or Jacob, the Servant is God's elected agent, with the divine Spirit on him (Isa. 42:1–2), and God gives him as a "covenant for the people, as a light for the nations." Similarly, Yahweh declares:

It is a great thing for you to be called my servant, to establish the tribes of Jacob and to bring about the return of the dispersed of Israel. See, I have set you forth as a covenant for the people, as a light to the nations, so that you might prove an instrument of salvation to the farthest corners of the earth (Isa. 49:6).

With Israel responsive to the Lord, the nations will hear of God's mighty salvation in her behalf. The very captives of Israel will bow down before her and say to God: "There is no other God. You alone are God, the Savior of Israel, only we did not know it" (Isa. 45:14-15). Others will say, "Righteousness and glory shall come to him, and all who separate themselves shall be ashamed" (45:24). Kings and princes will prostrate themselves before Israel in acknowledgment of God's salvation (49:6-7). Jerusalem (Zion) will be the center of this attention (40:9, et al.), when "all flesh shall see the salvation of God" (40:5), and her salvation will be a source of glory (46:13, *eis doxasma*), for the proclamation of salvation will be made, and God will reign for all to know (52:7-10; see also 59:20; 62:11; et al.).

Although it has been questioned whether the prophet anticipates conversion of the nations, there is no doubt that Luke understood the prophetic expectation as a pandemic statement, and certainly Isa. 51:4-5, if not 45:22, points in that direction: "A law shall go forth from me, and my judgment as a light for the nations. My righteousness draws near quickly, and as a light my salvation shall go forth, and in my right arm the nations shall put their hope" (cf. Psalm 97 [98]:2).

In any event, what happens to Israel is also to be a message to the nations that there is only one God—the Deliverer of Israel. Therefore the dispersed of Israel must divest themselves of their idolatry, adopted when they were captives, so that God's glory may be known among the nations. To that end the Servant of the Lord is dispatched on his mission.

The program will be difficult to achieve, for there are none so blind as Yahweh's servants, and none so deaf as those who lord it over them (42:19); nevertheless, God will endeavor to open the eyes of the blind (vv. 7, 16). For the people of Israel are to be witnesses to the uniqueness of Yahweh (44:8).

Jesus and Israel: Light-bearing Servants

Luke takes over the ambiguity inherent in Isaiah's figure of the Servant of the Lord, and much of the artistry of his work is related to his treatment of the subject. The story of Philip's encounter with the eunuch (Acts 8:26-40) is the most obvious exhibit for Luke's equation of Jesus with the Servant. But his total conception includes corporate Israel. Briefly stated: It is Israel's privilege to bear the light of God's salvation to the world. Jesus is the focus of God's salvation and calls Israel to share in the enterprise. Israel's hierarchy refuses, and Jesus selects others, the Twelve (Luke 6:12-15) and the Seventy (10:1-24), to assume Israel's burden. In the face of post-Pentecost resistance, it is apparent that Caiaphas's leadership will not assume the Isaianic assignment. Jesus therefore adds Saul-Paul to his staff for outreach to the nations. According to Isaiah, Israel is clearly the chief object of God's saving activity, with Jerusalem as the center of its celebration. In harmony with that perspective Luke concentrates on Israel and Jerusalem in his first two chapters. Luke's story begins with the annunciation to Zechariah in Jerusalem, followed by the announcement to Mary, with promise of an eternal reign for the Son of David (1:32–33). Both the Magnificat and the Benedictus stress themes of salvation, with the Benedictus culminating in the triumph of light over darkness (1:79). Near Bethlehem the shepherds see the effulgence of God's glory (2:9) and hear the angels "make proclamation" (*euaggelizō*) of news that spells "great joy." This consolation applies "to *all* the people" (v. 10), meaning, of course, all Israel, of whom the shepherds are representative recipients and also the first messengers (vv. 17–20). And the assumption is that once Israel recognizes the salvation in her midst she will serve as God's servant to the world.

To underscore Jesus' association with the hope of deliverance for Israel, Luke shows Jesus welcomed by two pious residents in Jerusalem, Simeon (2:25–35) and Anna (vv. 36–38); she spoke of God "to *all* who were looking for the redemption of Israel." In his twelfth year, Jesus returns to Jerusalem to affirm his identification with his heavenly Parent's purpose.

Since the Servant of Yahweh was to function with a view to the world's recognition of Yahweh, Luke shifts back and forth from Jerusalem to the larger world. The narrative of the birth of Jesus is preceded by a description of Caesar's census, and in keeping with a prophetic formula John the Baptist is introduced as a prophet within the context of civil and religious rule. Since all humanity is to see God's salvation (Isa. 40:3–5) Luke records a genealogy that links Jesus with all humanity (3:23–38).

In the temptation that follows (4:1–11) *all* the kingdoms are shown to Jesus (v. 5). But the last temptation presents us with Jesus in the temple in Jerusalem. This means that the achievement of his post as ruler of the nations will be accomplished in Israel's capital. Of course, this will happen in a way that only Simeon realized some thirty years earlier, after he had said of Jesus that here was "a light for revelation to the nations and the glory of your (God's) people Israel" (Luke 2:32; cf. Isa. 42:6; 49:6). All that remains after the recording of Jesus' temptation in the wilderness is for Luke to present Jesus as the active Servant of Yahweh, who brings salvation to his people and to the world; for salvation, as God's great benefaction, is Luke's commanding theme.

Luke 3:4–6 and 4:18–21

In contrast to popular apocalyptic expectations, Luke stresses that the long-awaited salvation made its appearance with the person of Jesus. Simeon took

God's salvation into his arms (Luke 2:30). Two other passages emphasizing this "now" aspect are of such a programmatic nature that they require attention before we proceed to analysis of Luke's treatment of traditions relating to Jesus as the pivotal point of God's salvation. The passages are Luke 3:4-6 and 4:18-21. (Luke's reason for shifting part of the OT quotation in Mark 1:2 to Luke 7:27 has already been discussed.) Thus it should be evident that Luke wishes to direct full attention to the Isaianic pattern of expectation.

In harmony with his motif of the exaltation of the lowly and humbling of the proud, Luke adds to Mark's quotation in somewhat modified form the words of Isa. 40:4 and closes with the words, *"all* flesh shall see the salvation of God" (Luke 3:6). These last words are in line with his understanding of Israel's mission as the bearer of light, or of knowledge of God's salvation, to the world. But equally significant is Luke's omission of a phrase immediately preceding these words in Isa. 40:5: "and the glory of the Lord shall be seen." Words along these lines appear in Luke's description of the light seen by the shepherds (2:9), but as an experienced fact, namely, "today." As a statement applying to the future the words, "the glory of the Lord shall be seen," would have been inappropriate at 3:5-6 because they might have suggested that the salvation of God would be presently experienced in the fiery apocalyptic of the type expressed in parts of the Book of Revelation. With his "today" in 2:11 Luke contemporizes God's salvation. This is the point also of 4:18-23.

The OT citation in Luke 4:18-19 moves from Isa. 61:1 to 58:6, and back to 61:2. Whether Isaiah 61 is to be classified as a "Servant" song or not cannot be determined here, nor is it important for our purpose. We seek to discover how Luke conceived the actual words and deeds of Jesus to be in continuity with the pattern of expectation expressed in the OT. With the help of the key phrase *pneuma epi* ("spirit on" someone) neither Luke nor his auditors would experience any difficulty in associating the words recorded at Luke 4:18-19 with the figure of the Servant of the Lord. That Luke attaches great significance to the words is clear from his repetition of their substance in Jesus' reply to John the Baptist's question at 7:22. That reply is directly linked with actions from John (v. 21). Therefore Luke 4:18-19 is to be understood as a definitive description of all that follows in Luke's narrative of Jesus' ministry. Luke accents the contemporaneity with the words, "and Jesus began to say to them, 'Today this Scripture has found fulfillment within your hearing!' " (4:21). Evidently this statement takes account of the consolatory character of the message (see Isa. 61:2); and consolation, as we noted above, is a vital part of the Servant's song.

At the beginning of his book, Luke drew attention to God as "Savior," the Supreme Benefactor, who raises up "a horn of salvation in the house of God's servant David" (Luke 1:69). The enemies from whom deliverance is expected are not defined at this point (v. 71). As an antidote to messianic misunderstanding, Luke gives prominence in 1:77 to the more general benefaction of forgiveness of sins. The announcement to the shepherds clearly indicates that the salvation described in the Benedictus (1:68–79) comes in connection with Jesus Christ. Until we come to 19:9 there is no further use of the term *sōtēr* (savior) nor *sōtēria* (salvation). Instead Luke uses the verbs *sōzō* (save) and *diasōzō* (rescue) to describe Jesus' conferral of salvation benefits especially on Israel. To these we now turn our attention, with particular reference to Luke's editorial activity, for attention has been paid in another context (pp. 32–39) to Jesus' healing activity.

Luke's Editing of the Theme of Salvation

Of such importance is the topic of salvation to Luke that he could not resist almost wholesale editing of his traditions. Out of all the instances in which he made use of Mark's material, he left only about five relatively untouched, including 6:9 (= Mark 3:4); 8:48 (= Mark 5:34, but see below); 9:24 (= Mark 8:35); 18:26 (= Mark 10:26); 18:42 (= Mark 10:52, but see below). Mark 3:4 pleased him because it is a capital text for his benefaction motif. Luke agreed heartily with Mark 8:35, for salvation is not of one's own doing. Similarly Mark 10:26 sets the stage for a repetition of the truth that salvation is God's miracle. Luke endorsed Mark 5:34, but his addition to Mark's v. 33 is in keeping with the motif of salvation that is made known to all: "she proclaimed it before *all* the people" (Luke 8:47). The word for "proclaimed" in this passage is *apaggellō,* Luke's favorite term for apostolic proclamation, and familiar to his Greco-Roman public from official decrees. In 18:42 he substitutes for Mark's *hypage* ("be off") in 10:52 the command "see again" (*anablepō*), with the verb repeated in Luke 18:43, thereby calling attention to the Servant's emphasis on recovery of sight to the blind (see 4:18, *anablepsis*).

Luke's additions to Mark, his introduction of non-Mark traditions, and also his omissions point further to the evangelist's interest in Jesus' life as expression of the Isaianic forecast of salvation. He added to Mark or introduced new material in the following references to salvation: 7:3, 50; 8:12, 36; (8:50); 13:23; 17:19; 19:10; 23:37, 39.

Five of the passages cited include recipients of physical benefits. The first of these, Luke 7:3, is a Q recital, which introduces the single occurrence in Luke's Gospel of the verb *diasōzō* (rescue). In keeping with Israel's mission as Servant of Yahweh is the introduction of the centurion's plea through "elders of the Jews." Through the intercession of Israel a "worthy" (7:4) Gentile receives the messianic benefit. Between Luke's lines: These elders do what all leaders in Israel ought to do.

The second, Luke 7:50, is an L recital. It contains the word of absolution announced to the sinful woman and connects faith and salvation. At 8:36, Luke altered Mark 5:16, "how things turned out for the man who was being controlled by a demon," to "how the one who came to be a demoniac was saved." At 8:50 he added the phrase, "and she shall be saved." Strictly speaking this is not an addition but a transfer from Mark 5:23. In this way, Luke created a link with the call to faith mentioned in Mark 5:36. He wished to emphasize that faith secures the benefit, just as the hemorrhaging woman had secured hers (Luke 8:48). The leper is assured at 17:19, an L account, that his faith has saved him. Salvation is spoken of in a more general way in three of the passages in which Luke makes additions to Mark's account.

At 8:12 Luke links faith and salvation through the added purpose clause: "in order that they might not believe and so be saved." The question, "Lord, are only a few being saved?" (13:23), gave Luke an opportunity to dismiss apocalyptic curiosity and to focus his public's attention on the importance of sincerity in profession of faith. The story of Zacchaeus (19:1–10) is an L recital, and 19:10 is probably an editorial comment on the saying that immediately precedes and again emphasizes the association of faith and salvation. Rhetorically it rounds out an artistically designed unit in which one seeker (Zacchaeus) is surprised by the Great Seeker. Salvation in these last three instances has to do with the experience of a new relation with God. In five of these passages Luke draws attention to the factor of faith. (On 23:37, 39, see pp. 53, 78).

Of interest also are Luke's omissions of Mark's detail. We have already spoken of his omission of part of Mark 5:23 at Luke 8:42. At 8:44 Luke omits reference to the woman's thought about getting healed by touching the hem of Jesus' garment (Mark 5:28), for he is more interested in showing that Jesus has "power" that derives from his Parent, and which is now active in the woman's behalf.

A tradition such as Mark 13:20 Luke could not use, because "all flesh shall see the salvation of God" (Luke 3:6), despite the fall of Jerusalem. Luke 21:28 therefore expresses Luke's two-phase apocalyptic and constitutes his correction of a misunderstanding that apocalyptic literalists might derive from Mark 13:20. Similarly, the form of Mark 13:13 is not precisely rendered in Luke 21:19, for salvation is available also as a present reality; instead, Luke offers a correlative form: "in your endurance you will gain real life for yourselves." At 23:35 Luke condenses Mark 15:29–32 (see Matt. 27:39–42). Naturally Luke 23:36 omits Mark's reference to Elijah (Mark 15:36). Mark 6:56 is part of the "Great Omission." Of interest also is Luke 8:24. In Matthew's parallel (8:25) the request "Lord, save us" is certainly Matthew's own addition to Mark 4:38. But even if Luke had found it in an allied source he would not have used it, for in 8:25 Jesus asks, "Where is your faith?"

From Luke's editorializing on Mark and related tradition, including additions and omissions, it is possible to confirm our understanding of what for him constituted salvation and how it is received:

1. Salvation is God's miracle, and may be experienced as a renewed relationship to God or as a specifically observed benefit from One who is kind to the just and to the unjust.

2. Jesus is the Father's channel of salvation power. Forgiveness of sins, the primary benefit, is the assurance of God's good will toward the individual.

3. Specific and observable benefits include especially (a) release from the power of Satan through exorcisms or healings and (b) restoration of sight.

4. Faith or repentance is a presupposition for the assurance of salvation as forgiveness and renewed relationship to God.

5. Faith may or may not be a presupposition for the receipt of salvation as a temporal benefit, such as healing.

6. The news of salvation is either communicated at the initiative of the recipient and bystanders, or by express directive.

7. Deliverance from the power of Satan is an aggressive demonstration of salvation-power.

8. Israel is the intermediary for God's communication to the Gentiles. Israel is the Servant of Yahweh, but Jesus is the Servant par excellence.

Silence Motif and Salvation

From the evidence presented, one may conclude that Luke is anxious to show that Jesus is the bringer of salvation promised especially by Isaiah. But what is to be said about his approach to Mark's silence (secrecy) motif? How successful is he in integrating it with his presentation of an open declaration of purpose such as the one delivered by Jesus at Nazareth? The fact that he retains most of Mark's references to a command of silence indicates that the motif was firmly embedded in tradition, otherwise he could have glossed over it completely. The pertinent passages in Mark are: 1:25, 44; 5:43; 7:36; 8:30; 9:9, 30.

In the recital of the first exorcism (Luke 4:33–37 = Mark 1:23–28) there is in fact no silence motif with respect to the publication of the healing. Only the demon is "muzzled," and this is part of the therapy, apart from the fact that Jesus would be understood as desiring no warrant from a demonic source. Luke's editorializing indicates that Satan's offer of *exousia* ("authority," 4:6) is countered by Jesus' own authority *and* by his *dynamis* (power), as v. 36 affirms, with emphasis on Jesus' word. In the surrounding area "every place" received report of the healing.

The order to the leper in Luke's account (5:12–16 = Mark 1:40–45) eliminates the word "nothing" (v. 44 in Mark) and retains Mark's emphasis on the "witness" aspect (v. 14). This would be in harmony with Luke's understanding of the function of Israel as recipient of divine benefactions. Hence Luke altered Mark's wording concerning the leper's apparent disobedience: "so all the more the story began to circulate," with the result that "many crowds came to hear him and to be healed of their diseases" (v. 15).

After the raising of Jairus's daughter (Luke 8:40–56 = Mark 5:21–43), Luke's account differs from Mark's in a number of details. First, Luke lays more emphasis on the fact that the young woman had died, for now her "spirit returned." Second, Luke shifts instructions about the giving of food to his description of her immediate resurrection, thereby emphasizing the permanence of her restoration to life. Third, in place of a vague subject "they were astounded," Luke says "her parents were astounded," with omission of Mark's Semitism. Fourth, with the subject for the verb "astounded" more clearly specified in Luke, the recipients of the instructions are now the parents, instead of Mark's bystanders. Fifth, in Luke the instructions are "not to tell anyone *what happened*"; in Mark, "No one is to *know this.*"

In addition to the points just observed, Luke introduced two changes of diction, *diatassō* ("direct") and *paraggellō* ("order"). "He *directed* that she be given something to eat . . . and he *ordered* the parents to tell no one what had taken place." Both these words are frequently used in bureaucratic circles. The changes are therefore of a piece with Luke's christological perspective and in keeping with the extraordinary demonstration of authority in the situation. Moreover, the verb *diatassō* is also a technical term for the making of testamentary depositions. Some of Luke's more perceptive readers would catch the double sense, a rhetorical device not infrequent in Luke's writing. Finally, it is to be observed that the verb *existēmi* does not connote a response of faith, but is rather equivalent in every passage in Luke-Acts to "they could not believe their eyes (or, their ears)."[1] To Luke the response of the parents would be inadequate for proper proclamation of the event (*to gegonos*), a term favored by historians and used by Luke for extraordinary occurrences (2:15; Acts 5:7; 13:12). They are therefore ordered not to say anything. Presumably it is to be inferred that the responsibility of communication must be left to qualified people, such as the apostles, of whom Peter, John, and James are representative.

At Luke 9:21, there is a slight alteration of Mark's "tell no one *about him*" (Mark 8:30) to "tell no one *this*," namely, that he is "The Christ of God." So as to give a clearer explanation for the order, Luke replaces Mark's "*and he began* to teach them . . ." with a circumstantial participle, "saying that. . . ." Thus he makes a tighter connection of the christological affirmation with the fate that is in store for Jesus in Jerusalem. Things have changed since the joyful news was given to the shepherds (2:11). In any event, the order does not concern anything that Jesus did. In the case of Mark 9:9, which states that Jesus instructed them not to report anything about what they had seen until after the Son of humanity's resurrection, Luke deletes the dominical order and simply observes that "they maintained silence and made no public proclamation in those days of anything they had (just) seen" (Luke 9:36). The initiative was theirs. As Luke is quick to point out, the majesty of God (9:43) is seen in the exorcism that follows on the very next day (vv. 37–43). This is the focus of the Servant's mission—his mighty deeds.

Also it must be noted that Luke immediately corrects any misunderstanding about the limitations of Jesus' openness in communication (cf. Mark 8:32). Whereas Mark 8:34–38, with its discussion of cross-bearing, is separated from the prediction of suffering (v. 31) by recital of the rebuke administered to Peter (vv. 32–33), Luke connects Jesus' saying about "daily" cross-bearing with the prediction of the Son of humanity's suffering by using the prefix: "And he was saying to *everyone*. . . ." (Luke 9:23). At the same time Luke shows that a confession of Jesus as God's Anointed One has no significance apart from one's personal identification with Jesus' fate. Luke's adoption of Mark's silence motif (Luke 9:21 = Mark 8:30) therefore actually provided Luke with an opportunity to exhibit an even clearer public enunciation by Jesus, and the pericope closes with an open declaration of the imminence of the kingdom of God. Some of Jesus' auditors "will not taste of death until they see the kingdom of God" (v. 27). That is, their cross-bearing will begin after Jesus' own death and resurrection have taken place. To be "the Christ of God" (9:20) means to be the one who is mocked at the crucifixion as "the Christ of God" (23:35), at which moment also the verdict will be displayed: "This is the King of the Jews." Indeed, none of them did die until they had seen the kingdom of God! Luke's addition to the succeeding narrative, concerning the conversation about Jesus' coming death in Jerusalem (9:31), continues the central theme of the answer to Peter's confession.

There are two instances of Luke's omission of Mark's secrecy motif. One of these is part of the "great omission" (Mark 7:36), of which account was made earlier. The other relates to Mark 9:30, which mentions a journey that Jesus did not want publicized. Of course, Luke cannot retain the passage, for at 9:51 he says that Jesus sent messengers ahead of him as he moved toward Jerusalem.

In one other passage there is a direct instruction to publish the news of a healing (Luke 8:39). By treating the secrecy motif as he has done, Luke is here able to avoid the problem raised by the apparent conflict of the directive in Mark 5:19 with other admonitions. Moreover, the open directive is of a piece with Luke's understanding of

Jesus' deeds as demonstration of the Servant's mission. In harmony with his views on divine benefaction Luke removed the ambiguity in Mark's expression, "the Lord," and wrote "God." Since Jesus gives expression to the Father's will, Luke retains Mark's conclusion: "he proclaimed what Jesus had done for him," only altering "in the Dekapolis" to "throughout the city." In Luke's work selected emissaries are responsible for systematic mission.

To summarize, Luke's treatment of Mark relative to the secrecy motif shows consistency in his disposition of the Servant motif. Jesus is committed to the objectives of Yahweh, and his mighty deeds are disclosed as an essential aspect of his identity as the Servant in mission to Israel and to the world. Since suffering is an essential aspect of the Servant's experience, Luke connects the question of his identity intimately with his future fate in Jerusalem.

The Climactic
Salvation-Demonstration

Between Luke 19:10 and the heart of the passion story there are no references to salvation, nor are there any healing miracles, except for the restoration of the slave's ear at 22:51. But in 23:35-39 there are four occurrences of the verb $s\bar{o}z\bar{o}$. In the first instance (v. 35), the leaders affirm what the Christian community knows to be the truth: "he saves others" (timeless aorist), but their concluding imperative turns their statement into a jest, "let him save himself." The soldiers speak in a manner appropriate to their profession: If Jesus is a king let him demonstrate it, "Save yourself!" Finally, one of the criminals says, "Save yourself and us." All of them misunderstand salvation. The Servant of the Lord cannot save others and at the same time save himself, for he has accepted the will of the Father as his own. In one of his parting words to the apostles he had said, "I am in your midst as one who serves" (22:27). The Greek words are different, but the way of the Servant of Isaiah 53 is the route whereby Jesus goes from profoundest humiliation to the heights of glory (see Acts 8:32-35).

The crucifixion is the climactic demonstration of Jesus' function as the Servant of the Lord. He is the glory of Israel, as Simeon had foretold, and by raising him from the dead God "glorifies" him (Luke 24:26) as the "one name under heaven whereby we must be saved" (Acts 4:12). Israel can now resume its mission as Servant to the nations. The twelve apostles are representative rulers in Israel (22:30), and their associates (24:33) are to go out with the proclamation of repentance in connection with the name of Jesus. Jerusalem is to be the first recipient of the consolation of the New Age. Just as Israel was called to function as witness before the world to God's salvation, so the recipients of the divine Spirit are to attest God's pardon in connection with the name of Jesus. Through the testimony of God's slaves, male and female, a new age of prophecy is to begin, with the objective that "*everyone* who calls on the name of the Lord shall be saved" (Acts 2:21).

Will it happen? Will Israel carry out its glorious privilege? Luke's auditors know that between the moment of the departure of Jesus from his disciples and the time in which the evangelist wrote his book the Servant's mission underwent severe testing. To this aspect of Luke's documentation and the importance that he attaches to repentance we now turn our attention.

Hardness of Heart

Failure to carry out God's intentions is a perennial topic in OT documents and finds expression in various metaphors that can be summed up in the expression "hardness of heart."

According to Israel's prophets, God's glory is evident through words (Deut. 5:24) and deeds (Exod. 16:6–7). The proper response to such divine words and deeds, or signs, is conviction accompanied by submissive worship (Exod. 4:30–31; cf. 14:31). There is to be constancy in acceptance of covenant responsibilities in view of the visible experience of Yahweh's saving acts (Exod. 19:4–5) and power (20:18–20). Similarly, the voice of God aims to secure obedience (Deut. 4:12–14). Yahweh is entitled to such fidelity, for Israel was delivered with a mighty hand out of Egypt (vv. 34–40). In contrast to blind and deaf idols (Deut. 4:28), God hears (cf. Exod. 2:24; Deut. 5:28; Zech. 7:11–13) and sees (Exod. 3:7, 9; 12:13; both seeing and hearing, Isa. 37:17). To participate in worship of idols means to partake of their character (Ps. 113:15–16 [115:5–6]), that is, to be blind and deaf, or, as Jer. 5:21–23 expresses the malady described in Deut. 32:6, to be guilty of folly and insensate rebellion. Persistent contrariness is the main symptom, of which Pharaoh is Exhibit A (Exod. 7:13). Alternate and interchangeable terms for this are stiffneckedness, crooked (perverse) generation, uncircumcised ear, uncircumcised heart. Isaiah 48:1–8 is a tour de force of metaphor, expressing the total impenetrability of the people in the face of God's words and deeds. Approaching it in rhetorical power is Isa. 29:13–24, which includes the contrasting combinations sight-wisdom and blindness-folly. Social irresponsibility goes hand in hand with rebellious deafness (Jer. 5:23–29) and blindness (Isa. 59:9–15).[2]

Even the Servant of the Lord, who fluctuates from an individual to a corporate figure, may be blind and deaf in his capacity as Israel (Isa. 42:18–20), that is, useless for service to Yahweh because he does not see God's works nor hear his words. Associated with the theme of hardness of heart is the understanding that divine retribution in the form of the same malady descends on the rebellious. Those who refuse to see or hear *shall* not see or hear. Since sight and hearing and their intellectual-spiritual counterparts are the gift of Yahweh, their absence is also to be traced to divine intervention. In this vein Deut. 29:4 observes: "The Lord did not give you a heart to understand, nor eyes to see, nor ears to hear until this day." In the same context, Israel is directed to heed the words of the covenant (vv. 18–19) and to make a life-death choice (30:15–20), while remembering that God circumcises the heart of the repentant (30:1–6). The classic statement of divine hardening is Isa. 6:9–10. But 29:13–16 points out that the retribution is not arbitrary, for the folly that pervades the people is the result of their own hypocritical religion and rebellion against Yahweh. Luke's Greco-Roman auditors would experience little difficulty in transposing all these Semitic modes of expression into their own cultural key, which had been sounded as early as Homer's *Iliad* (2.6). In an action similar to that of Yahweh's as recorded in 1 Kings 22:20-22, Zeus sends a deceptive heavenly messenger to Agamemnon. In a later time, and in a powerful mixed metaphor, the dramatist Sophokles has Teiresias say to Oidipous, "Blind you are in ears and mind and eyes" (371).

As the plaintive petitioner of Isa. 63:17 well knows, the doctrine of divine hardening is not irreversible. The same God who makes blind and deaf can also cure the malady. A strong note of consolation is implicit in this very stern belief. According to Deut. 30:1-6, God himself circumcises the hearts of those who return to the Lord their God in obedient recognition. Therefore the hard saying of Isa. 6:9-10 is put into fresh perspective by such a passage as 29:18: "The deaf shall hear in that day the words of a book, and the eyes of the blind that are in darkness and in gloom shall see." Again, "See, our God . . . will come and save us. Then the eyes of the blind will be opened and the ears of the deaf shall hear" (Isa. 35:4-5). The Servant has been given as a "light for the nations to open the eyes of the blind" (42:6-7). God "will lead the blind along a way they did not know . . . and will turn their darkness into light . . ." (v. 16); in the same vein, 61:1.

At a number of points in his two-volume work Luke presupposes acquaintance with some of the OT ground that has just been traversed. But it is necessary to divide his perspective into two parts. The one having to do with the validity of Jesus' credentials, the other with the Christian community's credentials as Servant of the Lord.

Jesus' Experience

Since Jesus is the Servant of the Lord in a distinguished capacity, it is anticipated that as the messianic deliverer he would open the eyes of the blind and the ears of the deaf. Various miracles indicate that he does so in a physical dimension not even anticipated by the Isaianic prophets. But these miracles point to a nonphysical dimension that *was* anticipated by them, namely, the preparation of Israel for obedience. In this latter respect, Jesus appeared to be a failure, for his own nation rejected him, and the question was asked whether instead of opening the eyes of the blind, he had not actually made apprehension of the truth difficult.

Chief evidence in that direction would have been his parables, and early Christians had a strong tradition that Jesus had spoken in parables "so that seeing they might not see and hearing they might not understand" (Luke 8:10; cf. Mark 4:12). Luke did not shy away from repeating the tradition—at 9:41 he even expands with Q on Mark 9:19 in the direction of phraseology in Deut. 32:5—and he agreed with the teaching implicit in it, that those who *will* not see *shall* not see. But he carefully prepared his public for the hard saying by showing through a series of incidents the hostility encountered by Jesus in the course of his outreach to Israel. And by incorporating the OT teaching at 8:10 he actually affirms the credentials of Jesus, for the words and deeds that give expression to God's salvation are characteristically met by hardness of heart (see also Acts 7). But that is not the last word. Luke makes a significant omission of Mark's concluding clause: "lest they be converted and receive forgiveness" (Mark 4:12). Luke is looking forward to Pentecost when the leaders of Israel will be faced with their crime; forgiveness *will* be available to the repentant. For them hardness of heart was to cease.

In the meantime deafness remains rampant. The rich man who, despite John the Baptist's warning (3:8), repeated the words "Father Abraham" to the very end (16:30) is told: "If they will not listen to Moses and the prophets, they won't obey even if someone were to rise from the dead." On his entry into Jerusalem Jesus says in patriotic tears: "If only you had known, my beloved city, the things that would have spelled peace for you. Alas, they have now been concealed (passive voice for divine action) from your eyes" (19:42).

The disciples are given "knowledge of the mysteries of the kingdom of God" (8:10). This understanding is, like its opposite, blindness and deafness of heart, the work of God. But even the disciples do not grasp everything about Jesus' role as Servant. On the other hand, just as knowledge is a divine donation, so lack of it is the result of divine intervention, "so that they might not perceive it" (9:45; similarly 18:34). In the same way the eyes of the two on the road to Emmaus "were held so that they did not recognize him" (24:16). But when he blessed the bread and broke it (24:30), in an action reminiscent both of the great bounty bestowed on the five thousand (9:12-17) and of his own self-giving (22:14-27), "their eyes were opened." They now remember the One who asked to be remembered. True understanding takes place in association with Jesus and through obedient listening to the Scriptures. Finally, it is Jesus himself who opens the mind to understand the Scriptures (24:45). That is the ultimate mission of the Servant, who was himself asked by a malefactor to be remembered.

Repentance

In the light of Luke's attention to the role of the Servant of the Lord and the past problems of Israel in apprehending divine purpose, one can better understand the meaning he attaches to repentance and what appears to be a contradictory note in 5:32 and 15:7.

Since the arrival of Jesus Messiah is at the same time the moment of Israel's greatest privilege, it is necessary that it be prepared for his coming. John is given that assignment (1:17), and he proclaims a repentance baptism (3:3). One must be prepared to undergo a shock to approved ways of thinking and action, standard social boundaryizing, ancestral cultic patterns, and routinized devotion to God—for new things are afoot, and without a revolution of the mind the New Age will be threatening to those who take refuge in ancestral securities (3:8). Without repentance on the part of the people, a Messiah who makes waves, crusades for the rights of outsiders, flaunts tradition, challenges the religious hierarchy, and democratizes God will speak as one speaks to those who have no ears.

Those who know their role as Servants of the Lord will have no problem. Together with Jesus they will know that it is their task to bring sinners to repentance. Of such it can be said that "those who are well do not require a doctor's services," for Jesus has not come to call the upright (*dikaioi*) to repentance but those who fail to attain the standard legal and cultic expectations (5:31). And this is part of the point of Luke 15. The Pharisees and scribes ought to be rejoicing with Jesus and God over the interest shown by numerous varieties of so-called undesirables in the reign of God. Instead, some grumble and complain that Jesus is on intimate terms with them (v. 2). And by their grumbling they betray their need of repentance. The Pharisee described in 18:9–14 was a model of uprightness (*dikaios*) and needed no repentance—that is, until he compared himself with other people.

Failure on the part of Israel's leadership to identify with the Servant pattern ultimately led to their rejection of the Great Servant. But, as Luke points out in Acts 3:17, they did it in ignorance, which is to say, they did not do it in willful disobedience against God. The door is open for a second chance to experience the messianic gift.

Second Chance

According to Isa. 43:8–10, the people of God are blind and deaf, yet they are brought forward as witnesses to the truth that Yahweh alone is entitled to divine honors. The ending of Luke's Gospel shows how the Servant-representatives of Israel have their understanding sharpened for the task that lies before them, namely to begin at Jerusalem with a worldwide mission. Just as Israel of old was to attest God's great deliverances in her behalf, so these Servants of the Lord are directed by the chief Servant to be witnesses to the great deliverance effected by God in connection with Jesus' life, suffering, death, and resurrection. Just as the Servant of Isaiah was given the Spirit of God (Isa. 42:1), just as Jesus the Servant was endowed with the Spirit (Luke 3:22; 4:18), so the Servants of the Servant are to await the gift of the Spirit in order to accomplish their assignment. The chief Servant will himself send the Spirit and thus administrate the promise of the Father (24:48–49).

At Pentecost the Spirit comes. Among other things, this means that the corporate aspect of the Servant figure becomes reality, and all the features of the New Age that were spelled out at Luke 4:18–19 are to be repeated in some form or another in the course of the apostolic mission. Of special interest is the fact that a second baptism involving repentance is proclaimed (Acts 2:38; cf. Luke 3:3). In an astounding display of beneficence God declares amnesty. The crucifixion will not be held against its perpetrators. Luke's editorializing is apparent in Peter's impassioned plea to Israel to accept God's offer of a second chance to share in the messianic benefits: " 'God's promise applies to you, to your children, and to all who are far away. . . .' He said many more things in his testimony and encouraged them in these words, 'Be saved from this perverse generation' " (Acts 2:39–40; see also 3:19, 22; 5:31). Typical elements here include: (1) universality of the messianic benefits; (2) God in supreme charge; (3) recognition of the reality of rebellion; (4) the message of consolation, that the rebellion is not irremediable (see also 4:10–12; 5:30–31).

Awareness of Luke's instruction on the second chance will go far in rescuing his interpreters from superficial assessments of his attitude toward Jews and Romans. The easy route is to conclude that he picks on Jews and lets Rome off the hook. But it is apparent from Acts 4:27, as well as from other passages, that Luke is neither hostile to Jews nor neutral toward Rome. Rome's puppet Herod and her administrative presence in the person of Pilate must assume their share in the judicial murder of Jesus. Yet there is no denying the fact that in the passion account the role of the Jewish hierarchy and its guilt predominates. Assuming that Luke was acquainted with Paul, if there was one thought that he gleaned from the apostle it was this: "Where sin abounded, grace did much more abound." But even without Paul, the Jewish Scriptures were sufficient generating sources for Luke's perspective. By permitting the guilt especially for Jewish leaders to dominate the passion recital, Luke sets the stage for the apostolic declaration of amnesty pronounced in Acts 2—4. In the same manner prophets of old recited the high crimes and misdemeanors of priests, administrators, and commercial interests as backdrop for God's munificent mercy. Given Luke's story of the proceedings, Greco-Romans who lacked acquaintance with the Jewish Scriptures would note the contrast between Jewish ingratitude for the gift of Jesus' presence among them and God's offer of opportunity for repentance, and they would be impressed by the magnitude of divine beneficence. A preview of such lavish beneficence had been offered by Jesus, who showed how forgiveness could move a flagrant sinner to a display of beneficence that challenged standard virtue (Luke 7:36–50; see also 19:1–10).

The Role of Israel and Rome

But how does one account for Luke's recognized tendency to focus attention on Jewish hostility toward the apostolic mission, while assigning an apparently laissez faire policy to Rome? It is to be noted, first of all, that Luke does include negative comment about some of Rome's provincial administrators.

For example, Paul does not hesitate at Philippi to insist on implementation of constitutional rights (Acts 16:16-40). Paul was not so successful with Felix (24:26), and had even less luck with Festus, who tried to use Paul as a political tool. The fact is, Paul cannot get fair treatment outside of Rome itself. In short, Luke does not denigrate the Roman constitution any more than he depreciates the constitution of Israel. But he takes to task violators of both. Indeed, Luke's treatment of Rome is far more complex than most of Luke's commentators have recognized. Secondly, the answer to the question posed above is to be sought at least partly in Luke's use of themes relating to the Servant of the Lord and the hardness of heart that inhibits some Israelites from carrying out the divine purpose.

Luke's account of Jesus' search for the lost (Luke 15) is again paradigmatic. The leaders of Israel should have shared the joy of Jesus in bringing outsiders back into the fold. And they should likewise have welcomed the apostolic outreach to the Gentiles. Instead, some among them encouraged attacks on developing communities of believers in the Messiah. This is the result of blindness to their responsibility as Servants of the Lord, and Saul of Tarsus is the prime exhibit of the malady. But he regains the sight he lost and becomes a paradigm of Israel as one who has been in default and then converted to the task of representing Israel in the role of the Servant (see esp. Acts 13:46-47, together with Barnabas).[3]

Those in Israel's leadership who remain in default of their obligation as the Lord's Servant oppose Paul and Barnabas in various parts of the world. For the most part, encounter with Roman officials is introduced as an antidote to charges that the Christians and their leaders foment public disorder or are engaged in activities that are subversive of Rome's interests. As in the passion narrative where the guilt of Israel was highlighted, in part to set the stage for the declaration of amnesty at Pentecost, so in Acts the hostility of Israel's leaders toward the apostolic mission is emphasized to contrast their default on the Servant mission and the apostolic fulfillment of it. Acts 28 appropriately ends with a statement about hardness of heart (v. 26), with Luke observing that some of the leaders believed Paul's message and others did not. But we are assured that Israel's assignment as such has not been left unfulfilled. "This salvation has been dispatched to the gentiles" (v. 28). The aorist affirms an accomplishment, not a resolution to ignore Jews. The words, "They will listen," are a statement of expected success and the final expression of a thematic term in the book.

At the same time that note is taken of Israel's default, interpreters of Luke's work must take account of the earnestness with which Luke confronts his Christian contemporaries. In effect, his work suggests two intersecting planes. The one conveys Israel with her failure to listen responsibly, and the other presents Christians who share to some extent the liabilities of Israel. The parable of the sower is therefore an expression of what Jesus encountered in his ministry and is at the same time paradigmatic of the apostles' mission and fortunes, for their activity is the continuation of what Jesus began to do and to teach (Acts 1:1). From Luke's editorializing it is clear that blindness among God's people was as real in Luke's time as in the time of Jesus. Only, says Luke, you cannot rid yourself of guilt by saying, "It's biblical Kismet; God has not chosen to have me see." No, you must face up, he says, to a twisted sense of values that sells out the solid stock of the kingdom for inflated trinkets and is ready to take a detour at the slightest sign of hazard on the kingdom-way. Therefore, to keep the church on its path Luke includes in the Gospel much that is embarrassing to the church, especially hypocrisy, partisan politics, and misuse of ecclesiastical position. Notable in Acts are the story about Ananias and Sapphira (Acts 5) and the warning issued by Paul at Miletos (Acts 20:17–38).

Luke aches with the Lord who shed tears over Jerusalem, and he would be the last to encourage anti-Jewish attitudes. Increased awareness of Luke's method in writing his history of Jesus and the church can therefore assist greatly in reducing the incidence of anti-Jewish sentiment that is based on misinterpretation of his work.

When the Seventy returned, exuberant after trying out the powers of the New Age, Jesus told them that it was more important that they have their names written in God's book (10:20). Evidently Christians are reminded by Luke that even while using divine resources they can become personally or institutionally apostate. Engagement in the task of proclamation is itself no guarantee that one's own ears are open to it. The priest and the Levite are not the only "bad guys" in the story of the Good Samaritan (10:30–37). It is sadly true that throughout the centuries there have been people who have called themselves Christians, and who have built up a reputation for adeptness in sins that were once associated by prophets and Jesus with Gentiles. And no other institutions in the history of the world have learned to be so competent in the art of excluding others as have ecclesiastical communities. It is not Pharisees who are asked, "Why do you call me, Lord, Lord, and do not do what I say?" (6:46). *Anyone* who comes to him gets the hard line, "Don't play games with me!"

Yet, while confessing their sin, Christians must avoid sentimentality and over-reaction to the guilt of churches and sects for their part in encouraging anti-Semitism. Caiaphas can never be taken off the hook by pinning all the rap on Pilate. The fact is, Caiaphas blew it. Nor are Pharisees picked out as whipping boys for the sins of early Christians any more than are James and John, who wanted to wipe out a Samaritan town with apocalyptic firebombs (9:54). To think that many Pharisees were not threatened by Jesus' revolutionary attitudes and methods would be an exercise in naïveté, unless, of course, one is prepared to reduce Jesus to a mouthpiece of the commonplace and view the alleged hostility as retrojection of Christian debates. In such event creativity of the kind ascribed to Jesus began with the church, and it is most certainly true that history has never repeated on that score! Is it at all credible that the early followers of Jesus would transmute an innocent Messiah into one who was rejected by the establishment in Jerusalem and then expend a great deal of intellectual effort to exonerate him? Apart from other historical considerations, it is more probable that the once-liberal Pharisaic sect succumbed to a liberal's chief temptation, to be resentful when being outliberalized.

In short, there are no "Christian" sins, and there are no "Jewish" sins. There are sins committed in the name of Christ that are of the same stripe that were responsible for the crucifixion of Jesus. Narrowness of mind, racial prejudice, resistance to alteration of traditions that isolate others from religious or constitutional rights, reservation of office, tribal vendettas, national arrogance, bigotry, and protection of turf that denies others access to public bounties—all are justly targeted as common debris. When Jews or Christians act like that they are not doing something invented by Jews or Christians. These are the games that the Herods, the Festuses, the Felixes, and the Pilates also play.

That Luke heightened the guilt of the hierarchy has been pointed out above, but he did so in order to set the stage for the apostolic declaration of a forgiveness that extends even to Israel's officials despite their part in the crucifixion of Jesus. On the third day God confronted his followers with the most astonishing surprise in all history by personally exonerating Jesus. Now all Israelites and all humanity must readjust their thinking, that is, repent. Which is worse, Luke would ask: Caiaphas who played games with Pilate in a vain attempt to abort history, or Peter, who tried to save his skin when the destiny of humanity was turning on its hinges?

In order that Christians might not so historicize the gospel material that it becomes irrelevant for their own decision, Luke uses various editorial devices to remind his public that they are not to forget to find themselves first of all in the gospel tradition. The evangelist may therefore shift from dialogue between the crowd and Jesus (12:1–21) to a personal exhortation given by Jesus "to the disciples" (see, e.g., 12:22). "Do you mean us or everyone in that parable?" asks Peter at 12:41. "Pharisees" hear the parables about God on the search (chap. 15), and also the one on the rich man and Lazarus (16:19–31), but in Luke's time the words about Pharisees function as a mirror before one's face. Jesus scorches "his disciples" with warnings about offenses, erring associates, and the "what a good fellow am I" complex (17:1–10). At 17:22 the participants in dialogue with Jesus shift from Pharisees to disciples, with emphasis on the problems of a community imperiled by dissension on matters having to do with apocalyptic schedules.

With such and sundry other rhetorical devices Luke relates the Jesus of history to the history of his followers. Ultimately it is the church, not Pharisees or others from the past, with which Luke is concerned. For the Pharisees themselves are not a monochromed caricatured group. Some of them are hopelessly stuck in tradition, but others warn Jesus about Herod (Luke 13:31); they are not involved as a group in the crucifixion of Jesus; and some of them become believers in Jesus (Acts 15:5). Rather, Luke's chief concern is that Christians remain on target with respect to their Servant-mission. To help the church adapt to change is one of the theologian's chief tasks. In Luke's time inherited forms of faith were on a collision course with the challenge of a New Age. The gospel genre provided Luke the opportunity to put various traditions into proper perspective and at the same time make Jesus contemporary with the church and the church contemporary with Jesus, and both contemporary with the future.

As Luke well perceived, the freedom of Jesus—with respect especially to sabbath tradition—and the destruction of the temple in the year 70 were historical correlatives. The realm of the sacred had expanded to embrace the world.

CHAPTER SEVEN

JESUS—THE PERSON

Detailed analysis of Luke's Christology runs the risk of removing Jesus from the everyday history of humanity. Likewise, anxiety about repeating the errors of nineteenth-century "liberal lives of Jesus" may lead to a depreciation of the "human" dimension of Luke's record of aspects of the life of Jesus. It is easy to forget that whereas "Christ" and "Lord" are titles, it is the term "Jesus" that expresses the full weight of concern for humanity's rescue. It is the ONE NAME (Acts 4:12). Throughout what follows, one should note that Luke's projection of Jesus is under view.

What Jesus said and did was of a piece with what he was intrinsically as a person—totally and radically committed to Yahweh's will and purpose and to the liberation of people. That unique aspect of his *life* was of such interest to Luke that it serves as the nerve center for his total christological construct. For the future of Christianity depended, so far as Luke was concerned, on fidelity to the radicality in Jesus' own personal style of life, word, and action. But in that very radicality there were depths of human expression of such admirable quality that they would appeal to gentile admirers of the highest virtues, who might otherwise have had little interest in the subtler points of theology.

Deep Loyalty

Acquainted with a world of shallow relationships based on narrow reciprocity principles (Luke 6:32–35), Luke first of all appears to have been impressed with Jesus' loyalty both to God and his associates.

Filial Piety

Luke's portrait of Jesus as one intensely devoted to his Father's purpose makes an impact of theological and psychological unity.

Demands of historical rhetoric may have been a formal cause for the inclusion of a story about Jesus' precociousness at the age of twelve (Luke 2:41–52), but this incident, with its emphasis on Jesus' commitment to his heavenly Parent, is of a piece with all that follows. Identified by the voice from heaven as God's Son in whom the good will expressed to the shepherds (2:14) finds embodiment (3:22), Jesus is given genealogical identity with Israel and with all humanity, as far back as Adam, and through Adam again to God (3:23–38).

Fiercely loyal to his Father's will expressed in Deuteronomy, Jesus accepts a death-time assignment of battle with God's chief political adversary (4:1–13). Reflecting such prior commitment are the repeated references to the driving force of necessity that was first expressed at 2:49. Despite the threat on his life at Nazareth (4:29–30), he insisted on going ahead with the proclamation of the kingdom, because "God sent me for this purpose" (4:43; the passive voice in "I was sent" implies God as agent). His death is similarly presented, not as the death of a tragic hero, but as the goal of one who knows what he must do (13:33). The passion predictions about the Son of humanity are in harmony with that determination (9:22; 17:25; 22:37). Jesus has messianic qualifications not only because what happened to him is in harmony with the Scriptures, but because he himself was committed to his heavenly Parent in such a way that his existence becomes the medium for understanding the Scriptures. Thus Luke's resurrection narrative displays interest in both the personal commitment of Jesus (24:7) and the theological and apologetic interest of the people of God (24:26, 44). In the face of the most critical hour known in all history, Jesus had not flinched (22:42).

At about the same age that Alexander the Great was when he died, Jesus the Great (1:32) put into the Father's safekeeping the *pneuma* (spirit) that had endowed his unique life (23:46). It had never parted from him, not even in the darkest hour. Alexander died with worlds yet unconquered, but Jesus would, within a few weeks, share that Spirit with the disciples, who would bring his name to *all* nations (24:47).

Such strength of commitment found nourishment in the hills of Galilee. Constantly in touch with his Father, Jesus never loses the road. And Luke, by his very choice of many scenes in which he displays Jesus at prayer, shows that his hero never forgets the task to which he subscribed. All the moments in which Jesus prays to his Father are in contexts that suggest hostility to Jesus, or at least a threat of hazard.

Far from being a populist, Jesus communes with his Father before selecting his twelve cabinet members, and this after scribes and Pharisees were beside themselves with fury over his healing of a man with a paralyzed hand (6:6–11). Ironically, Judas, their volunteer hit-man, was included in the list (v. 16). The words of 9:16 will have their echo in the night of Jesus' betrayal (22:19).

The transfiguration is connected with prayer (9:28), and well it might be, for the context is punctuated with references to Jesus' death. At 9:51 Jesus heads with determination toward Jerusalem. At 11:1 he is praying, and the context sets up the dramatic opposition of true vs. false spirit. The enemy says that Jesus works with Beelzebul (11:15), and after this scene there comes a long series of warnings and exhortations, until finally Jesus is again praying— this time on his knees, in a gesture of climactic commitment. He is about to lift to his lips a cup that never held such bitter dregs (22:42)—but he will drink it, and with it a health to the world. He who had been watching Satan plummet to earth (10:18) and "in that very hour" had himself affirmed what a paradoxical Father he had—but a Father who knew what had to be done—now meets his foe in full command of the situation (22:45-53).

Loyalty to His Associates

Despite the miserable treatment he receives from some of his closest friends, Jesus remains fiercely loyal. This characteristic of Jesus displayed in various traditions struck Luke so profoundly that he gave prominence to the contrasting pattern in the passion narrative. The male disciples fight for kingdom-advancement in ways that suggest they had scarcely heard a word Jesus said (22:24-27; see 9:46-50). After rebuking them, Jesus magnanimously expresses appreciation for their loyalty and promises them a kingdom with access to his royal table (22:28-30).

In related fashion, Luke displayed the constancy of Jesus in the face of Peter's anticipated denial and the ridiculous behavior of his disciples (22:31-34). No band of followers could have been more knuckle-headed than the eleven apostles who came equipped to the final battle with two swords (22:38) and ended up slashing off a piece of ear (22:50). Luke may have known the culprit's name, but kept his pen dry; John's Gospel blows the man's cover (John 18:10-11). In any event, Jesus, in a further demonstration of his care for "little people," repaired the damage and the plot moves on. Standing on the one side is Peter pleading for every hair on his own head and every ounce of blood in his body: "I never knew this guy. . . . No, I don't move in that crowd. . . . You're crazy!" (22:54-60). The words are scarcely out and the rooster crows. While Peter weeps bitterly, Jesus endures the buffoonery of the guard, and within a few hours, unlike Peter, he tells the truth and seals his doom (22:66-71). But he could count on his female disciples. They took the dangerous route (23:55).

Confident of success, Jesus assured his followers they had nothing to fear. They were worth more than sparrows (12:7; cf. 21:18; Acts 27:34). Yet he did not spare them from the ultimate sacrifice for taking up common cause with him (Luke 9:23-27). On the other hand, there might be times when, like Peter, some of them lost their nerve, but he would not forthwith renounce them nor denounce them (12:10).

In his last moments he might have removed some of the cloud of insurrection and rebellion that had come over him because of his unorthodox style of life, but true to his mission he remained the friend of publicans and sinners. In almost his last breath the Great Benefactor identified one of the malefactors with his own fortunes. Paradise was thought to be reserved for the righteous. But he told the malefactor that both of them would share the place that very day. This was the rarest loyalty.

King

Regal Poise

So far as Luke was concerned, Jesus was born to command, and the evangelist was also impressed by the regal poise that Jesus combined with human touch. Completely in control of any situation, Jesus slept soundly through a raging storm but could not withstand the battering of his disciples' fearful voices (8:22–25).

Caesar once quelled a rebellion in the ranks of his soldiers with a single word, "Quirites" ("Citizens"). He was letting them know that his seasoned veterans were out of uniform, looking like recruits fresh from the Roman forum. Residents of Nazareth tried to run Jesus off a cliff. He did not run, but went right through their ranks (4:29). Jesus would die in his own and God's good time.

Luke knew about kings and preparations for war (14:31–32). But no king made more careful preparations than did Jesus, nor did he underestimate his enemy. Rashness was held in contempt by prudent generals. Jesus respected the odds that faced him, and he was on his knees in Gethsemane. But there was no bending when he stood before Caiaphas and Pilate.

Regal Generosity

This king did not hold people off at arm's length. He broke taboos without fear of consequences when he put his hands on the sick (4:40; 13:13), made personal contact with lepers (5:13), and touched dead bodies (8:54). Unimpressed by the name-dropping games that society plays, Jesus placed a child near himself and made association with himself dependent on a total change of values (9:47).

On his way to Nain he met a funeral cortege coming out of the village (7:11–17). So impressed was Luke by this scene that he speaks of Jesus as "The Lord." At the very frontier of human existence Jesus is in sole and supreme command. In keeping with his literary tact of reserving reference to Jesus' emotions for exceptional instances (see 19:41–46), Luke observes that Jesus "had compassion" for her. This is the ultimate that humanity can display in the face of a disaster of such magnitude as death, for as Zebulon 7:3 of the *Testaments of the Twelve Patriarchs* observes: "When you are unable to help the person in need, at least be compassionate and filled with pity." But King Death has met his match. Here is one whose compassion is the prelude to action. "Weep no longer!" Head on into the face of death he marches, touches the pallet, and gives the royal command: "Young man, I order you to get up!" Out of divine compassion the "Daystar" was to "visit" those who were sitting in the shadow of death (1:78–79). The crowd acknowledges that God had paid a visit to their little town (7:16). And some of Luke's Greco-Roman auditors would recall how Herakles harrowed Hades to bring Alkestis, wife of Admetos, back from the haunts of the dead.

In the other two cases where Luke uses the verb "have compassion," he likewise associates it with mercy in the face of death. The Good Samaritan rehabilitates a man left "half-dead" (10:33) and the prodigal's father has pity (15:20) for a son who "was dead and had come to life" (15:32). Of course, from this latter illustration about the "welcoming father" we know what Luke meant by his inclusion of the story of the resurrection at Nain. All who repent will hear the voice of the King who invites them to the Great Banquet Hall.

Regal Hospitality

Since his traditions were full of references to Jesus' sociability, Luke had no difficulty in adjusting his sources to the Hellenistic rhetorical technique of using banquets as scenic backdrop for recording of a great man's thoughts on various subjects. From the varieties of social classes that found representation in his company, it is clear that Jesus projected a spacious hospitality. Like his party-giving Parent (Luke 15), he loved a social hour and it is fair to assume that if he could "let loose" with Spirit-filled ecstatic prayer (10:21) he did not recline with his friends in the somber mood so often associated with him in the long history of religious pictorial representation. People of that stripe are not invited back!

To royal manners born, he moved with ease among the high and the low. Regardless of the precise circumstances, Luke's recital of Jesus' encounter with a Pharisee and a notorious woman who had crashed his party (7:36-50) displays the historian's sensitivity to distinctive aspects of Jesus' personality. Jesus was not contemptuous of the wealthy and the respected. He was neither aloof nor class-conscious. He accepted invitations across the board, for to a king all are commoners. Ultimately, he considered quality of relationships more significant than arbitrary classifications due to accidents of birth or social history.

Secure in his relationship to Yahweh, Jesus did not purchase artificial status at the expense of human feeling. He was a gentleman, with manners not turned on to standard expectation. And so he said of the woman whose sensitivities the rude host had punctured with hypocritical volleys, "Look at all her kindnesses. As a hostess she has done better than you. As for her sins, I grant you, they are many, but she has already received forgiveness. Love like hers does not go hand in hand with sin." Then he said to the woman, "God has forgiven you" (7:48). It was not the "polite" thing to say, but the kingdom took precedence over the socially "correct things." With his concluding words in v. 50 Jesus sends the woman off in possession of far more class than his host had displayed.

"God exalts the humble and brings down the mighty" (1:52). Jesus lived in the light of that truth, and because it was his way, Luke expresses the theme throughout his work. Against the backdrop of fussy interest in being seen in the right places and in the right garb, Luke shows how Jesus transmutes a widow's worth into astronomical figures and lets the bottom drop out of the market for the rich (21:1–4) who have exploited her religious sensitivities.

This widow was only one of many women noticed by Jesus. In an age when there was not much less sexism than in our own, Jesus, having no hangups himself about sex, related to women with ease. His courtly manners, his genuine interest, his sensitive consideration and profound respect for womanhood attracted large numbers of women who shared his own commitment to service (8:1–3; 22:27). He showed that women need not be defined in terms of a specific line of work, and he complimented Mary for being an excellent scholar (10:38–42). While cowardly males remained at a safe distance (23:49; 24:33), some of these women (24:10) watched carefully where their king was to be buried (23:55). Only with the barriers of caste and class broken by one like Jesus could Luke have gone on to describe the meeting of the expectant Christian community—the very first after Jesus' ascension—as one of complete collegiality between male and female (Acts 1:12–14). Institutionalized churches would in the centuries to come diligently work to ensure that this collegiality would be recognized as a very temporary state of affairs, relegated to the beginnings of Christianity but not normative for the church's life.

Luke well knew how protocol and diplomacy could drive a court's social bureau frantic. One mistake in seating and a country might be at war. With Jesus he was amused by the ridiculous sight of grownup people jockeying for recognition at social events, so he reports Jesus' lecture on good manners (14:7–14). Luke was profoundly aware of the sociology of tyranny and the intimate connection between habits of everyday social grace and the grace of God. Jesus simply made a daily habit of that grace, which was his to a remarkable degree already at the age of twelve (2:40, 52).

Regal Perspective

Partly because he did not wear his crown too heavily, Jesus was able to rise above attacks and disappointments of varied magnitude. Without humor not even God can survive. Jesus did not much appreciate the religiosity that viewed the Creator as a dour-faced bookkeeper (19:21) and, unlike the zealot who is usually not much for laughs, he punctuated his repartee with lively humor. The shepherds were promised a world with joy (2:10). Luke's Jesus did not come to put a damper on it. When told by some Pharisees that Herod was out to kill him, Jesus said, "Tell that fox, the hen will not be intimidated." Commentators have debated a long time what Luke's Jesus meant by calling Herod a fox. The clues are all there in 13:31–35.

Hilarious is the picture of a man with a plank in front of him trying to pull out a splinter from another person's eye. Yet more hilarious is the effort made in the course of interpretive history to "explain" Jesus' joke recorded in 18:25. Yet even a child knows the answer. It's not the camel, but the hump!

In the presence of his Father, Jesus was equally at ease, and the prayer ascribed to him in 10:21–22 conveys a subtle humor reflecting the life of one for whom Yahweh spelled joy not gloom. To a person aspiring for empty goals of achievement, experience of the kind of misunderstanding, hostility, and injustice that constantly confronted Jesus would be frustrating. But Jesus sensed the humor in it and said to his Father, "The stupid see and the wise go blind. Well, that's the way you want it." And a centurion finally said, "This was a just and good man."

Plutarch relates that Otho, one of the three emperors who reigned between Nero and Vespasian, expressed concern for his soldiers in the face of certain defeat with these words:

> All persons may be equally subject to the caprice of fortune, but of one thing it cannot deprive good men, that is, to act reasonably under misfortune.

Jesus exceeded the limits of expectation. Gabriel had predicted his greatness (1:32). The centurion's verdict on Jesus' life, "This was an upright and innocent man" (23:47), echoes what the Hellenistic world valued most, namely excellence of the highest order, featuring especially magnanimity and integrity, the marks of a truly great benefactor. At the beginning of his Gospel, Luke had associated Jesus with upright people, including Zachariah and Elizabeth (1:6), pious Mary (v. 38), the faithful shepherds (2:8–17), patient Simeon (2:35), and loyal Anna (vv. 36–38). And at the end there appears the "good and righteous" Joseph of Arimathea (23:50–53). The centurion's verdict sets the tone for identification of Jesus as the "just" one in Acts (3:14; 7:52; 22:14), and his sense of perception puts him in the same rank with the centurions of Luke 7:1–10 and Acts 10:22. Jesus was not one of yesterday's people.

PART 4

"FOLLOW ME"

CHAPTER EIGHT

ETHICS AND THE GOSPEL

Tightly integrated with Luke's Christology is his concern about the moral and ethical implications of the good news. Indeed, a superficial analysis of Luke's moral theology might suggest that about the best ethical advice he can give is to be good and love your neighbor, and that what he presents as approved morality is on the whole impractical and an invitation to individual or corporate suicide.

Such a conclusion would obviously be unfair, for Luke does not pretend to present an ethical treatise, nor does he personally engage with his traditions in explicit editorial dialogue. At the same time, the question must be asked: Is Luke's approach to the moral implications of Christianity, as he knows it, integrated with the rest of his presentation, and especially so in the Gospel?

Repentance/Conversion

In part 3 it was observed that Luke views repentance as a change of mind that is prepared to entertain the surprises and possibilities of the New Age. Without such altered thinking the immensity of God's revolutionary display of beneficence could not possibly be appreciated. Those who, like Simeon, unconditionally welcome Jesus as God's unique gift, have no problem. Others must face the need of profound changes in their thinking.

The newness of the age that dawns with the arrival of Jesus is such that the mind itself must undergo a revolution. Luke terms it "repentance" (*metanoia*; verb, *metanoeō*) and also uses the synonym, "conversion" (*epistrophē*; verb *epistrephō*). The rich man who calls on Abraham three times in 16:19–31 is a prime exhibit of failure to alter one's thinking and share in God's outreach to the disadvantaged and the dispossessed. He discovers to his sorrow that time for repentance is limited. He ought to have revised his thinking in accordance with the injunctions of Moses and the prophets (vv. 30–31), who have much to say about justice and responsibility for the poor. And time was running out for his brothers.

But what about the publicans and sinners? Such is the beneficence of God that it reaches out also to them, for remission of sins, as Zachariah proclaims, is a central feature of the New Age (1:77). And they too are told that they must alter their thinking. There is no patronage in John's forthright proclamation (3:10–14).

The story about Zacchaeus (19:1–10) provides fuller exposition of John's preaching. There are three stages in his experience of Jesus as the focal point of the beneficence of God in the New Age. (1) Jesus affirms his necessary (*dei*, v. 5) commitment to the mission of God. Much of the prevailing religious system encouraged the recognition and maintenance of distance between God and humanity. Luke notes the extent to which ritual apartheid penetrates society. He makes no special mention of priests or leaders of the people, but states that "*all* murmured" (v. 7), for through his self-invitation ("I must stay at your house today") Jesus struck a decisive blow against everyone's version of cultic boundaryizing. This meant that all were in need of a revolution of their minds if they were to understand what was afoot "today." (2) That the distinguished prophet from Nazareth should grace the abode of Zacchaeus and in the process put his own reputation at risk was such a display of courageous beneficence that Zacchaeus was drawn into the very vortex of repentance (see v. 8). (3) Since Zacchaeus laid no claim to genetic privilege and so did not violate John's injunction (3:8–9), but did "bear fruits that befit repentance," Jesus affirms him to be a descendant of Abraham. This redefinition of what constitutes Israel was to have far-reaching implications for the world-thrust of the apostolic mission. According to John's father, God had sworn to rescue Abraham's descendants (1:73–74). Luke's story about Zacchaeus twice calls attention to salvation (19:9–10). Deliverance from "all who hate" them is included in Zachariah's song (see 1:71). One of the most hated was saved one day in Jericho.

To understand Luke's view of Gentiles relative to the question of repentance, it is necessary to distinguish between those who have made the acquaintance of the one true God and those who are still guilty of deviant worship. In the first group belongs Cornelius (Acts 10—11; see esp. v. 2), whose alter ego is portrayed in Luke 7:1–10. The account of Peter's visit with Cornelius is vital to the unity of Luke's work. Peter's response to Cornelius will determine whether Israel displays in this apostolic representative the kind of conversion or readiness to question one's traditions that is required to implement the kind of pandemic outreach that Jesus exhibited in his own ministry, when he ate and drank with publicans and sinners. By accepting Cornelius' invitation to his home and company, Peter gives dramatic evidence of his own repentance or total change of viewpoint on cultic matters (Acts 10:28–29). Luke goes on to show that the acceptance of Cornelius is based on Peter's perception of divine beneficence. God shows no partiality (v. 34), and Jesus reflected the divine beneficence, for he himself was a benefactor (*euergetōn*) who healed "*all* that were oppressed by the devil" (v. 38). In effect, Luke himself offers one of the fundamental reasons for his peculiar treatment of the healing stories in his Gospel; they are stories about Jesus' benefactions.

By raising the crucified Jesus from the dead, God validated Jesus' earthly ministry, which had violated some cultic restrictions. This means that God declared many former cultic procedures obsolete. In line with prophetic testimony, relations with God are determined by one's recognition of Jesus as the one through whom forgiveness is received (Acts 10:43). Gentiles who "fear" God and "do what is right" (v. 35: *ergazomenos dikaiosynēn*, that is, function as benefactors) are welcome to share in all the rights and privileges that were ever extended to the chosen people. Cornelius qualifies, and in confirmation thereof the Holy Spirit fell on him and "*all* who heard the word" (v. 44). At this point Luke refers to Jews as the "circumcised" (v. 45). With this choice of term Luke signals a dramatic moment, for Peter goes on to speak about baptism. The "circumcised" were amazed, but Luke, who relates hostility of Jews on many other occasions, evidently here views them as casting their vote in support of the proceedings. In any event, baptism in the name of Jesus succeeds circumcision as an indicator of legitimate peoplehood before God. A revolution has taken place, and the succeeding chapters in Acts relate the consequences of Peter's own exhibition of the fruits of repentance; for example, Peter takes the initiative in exhorting the apostles and elders to liberalize for Gentiles the means of entry into God's family (15:6–11). How little did the first audience of John the Baptist grasp the implications of a "baptism" of repentance for the forgiveness of sins" (Luke 3:3; Acts 13:24)!

But what about Gentiles who have not previously recognized the God of Israel? According to Luke, the inference to be drawn from the story about Cornelius is that God is prepared to bestow life on all who repent. From a Jewish-Christian perspective this means, on the one hand, the renunciation of deviant worship and the immorality traditionally associated by Jews with such worship; and, on the other hand, faith in Jesus as God's definitive demonstration of divine goodwill. Repentance will therefore mean for Gentiles a break with cultic traditions that were as deeply embedded as the rite of circumcision was for Jews.

Luke's mode of reinforcing the link between Jewish and gentile experience in the face of divine beneficence is the use of recitals relating to lame persons. At Luke 7:22, Jesus called attention to his healing of the "lame" as a primary mark of his credentials. At Jerusalem, the healing of a lame man initiates a series of encounters with the Jewish populace (Acts 3—4). Similarly at Lystra, the healing of a cripple dramatizes the impact of the Christian message in gentile territory (Acts 14:8–18). Both groups, Jews and Gentiles, are thus confronted with displays of divine beneficence effected through Jesus, and in both instances the broader concern of God is connected with the specific beneficent action. Acts 4:9 refers specifically to the healing as a *euergesia* (benefit) and then puts it in the context of a more general message of salvation (v. 12). Likewise, the balance of Luke's report of Paul's message to the crowds at Lystra links the specific benefit of healing with God's providential and merciful *benefaction* for humanity. For both Jews and Gentiles, repentance is essential to receipt of the larger benefit. Israel is to repent in response to God's new beneficence that has been exhibited in the resurrection of Jesus. The people of Lystra have witnessed the beneficence of the Maker of all things. Despite their lack of appropriate recognition, God has been merciful. But now it is time to turn from their vain devotions to the worship of the "living God." In Luke's narrative the people recognize the connection between the message about the Supreme Benefactor (14:17, *agathourgōn*) and the healing of the lame man—they display repentance (*epistrephō* is the verb, v. 15) by showing their gratitude to the agents of beneficence (v. 18). Paul and Barnabas try to redirect their thinking, even as Peter had done at Jerusalem (see Acts 3:12). That they were at least partially successful can be inferred from the reference to Christian assemblies in vv. 22–23.

Luke's record of Paul's speech at Athens (Acts 17:22–31) includes a further example of how intimately Luke associates divine beneficence and repentance, and at the same time shows that God can be worshiped without traditional cultic process. Stephen had demonstrated that Israel could do without a temple (7:47–50), and Gentiles learned that they can do without shrines (17:24–25). Paul's theme of a beneficence that encounters ingratitude is graciously expressed with the observation that the offense has taken place in "times of ignorance" (v. 30). So had Jews also been admonished for their failure to recognize God's beneficence in the life and ministry of Jesus (3:17). From all this it is apparent that Paul's observation about the Athenians' religiosity (17:22) was an allusion to their efforts to be responsive to the benefactions of many deities. Repentance (v. 30) means a shift from misdirected responsiveness to divine beneficence. Since "righteousness" is a dominant factor in the definition of beneficence, Luke says God "will judge the world in righteousness (*en dikaiosynē*) by a man whom he has appointed, and of this God has given assurance to *all* by raising him [i.e., Jesus the Just (*dikaios*)] from the dead" (v. 31; cf. Acts 3:14; 7:52; 22:14). By emphasizing the resurrection of God's special deputy, Luke also invokes the Greek conception of Immortals—who win immortality because of their benefactions—for better perception of Paul's tactics in dealing with an Hellenic audience.

In sum, the port of entry into the benefits of the New Age is by repentance, by a revolution in heart and mind. It is a conversion, that is, faith in God's action in Jesus Christ—a benefaction for all. For Jews, response to the apostolic proclamation would mean the ratification of one who was disqualified by the highest religious authorities. To Gentiles it would mean acknowledging mastery of the world to one who was rejected by his own people and sentenced by a Roman prefect to a death reserved for malefactors. In either case, vast readjustments of personal attitude and performance go hand in hand with a claim to be that same man's follower and devoted servant.

Since repentance takes place in a variety of ways, and since the expectations of God leave no room for contradictory loyalties, the call to repentance does not invite a phony confession of sin. To qualify for the benefits of the New Age, it is not necessary for "good" Israelites to confess long lists of vices of which they are not guilty, for Jesus has not come to call the righteous to repentance. Nor need the "god-fearers," that is, Gentiles who find Israel's religion attractive, come up with sins they never even thought of committing. Rather, the call to faith in Jesus Christ would be all the more shocking in its demand to a morally respectable person than to a disreputable one precisely because the reputable would be invited to have their lives called into question by association with one who died in disrepute. Indeed, the more reputable they were, the more difficult would they find continual association with this one who set society on its head by his weird style of life and by his unreasonable and impractical demands. A disreputable person, on the other hand, might be attracted to the first-class citizenship he or she could receive in the eyes of God, but would find the response of someone like Zacchaeus a hard act to follow. In any event, the apostles were not apologetic about their proclamation. Good or bad, repentance (*epistrephō/metanoia*) meant "performance worthy of a claim to being repentant" (see Luke 3:8; Acts 26:20).

Entry into Liberation

Repentance meant that one became a beneficiary of "salvation." One of the chief functions of Jesus as Savior was release of the world from its bondage to darkness (Luke 1:78–79). Not much good is to be said for darkness, and Satan is closely associated with it. Those who try to play both sides of the street with God must face the fact that even the light within them is darkness (11:34–35). Luke 22:53 expressly says that the apprehension of Jesus took place at a time assigned for the power of darkness. From the evangelist's reference to Satan at 22:3 we know who the administrator of darkness is, and Acts 26:18 explicitly identifies recovery of sight with a turning away from the authority of Satan to the authority of God.

What Luke in effect describes is a conflict between the claims of God over human existence and the counterclaims of forces, institutions, and environmental factors that deprive people of their right to function as God's people, rob them of identity, and reduce them from persons to statistics. That his thought moves along such lines is suggested by his presentation of Jesus' passion in which Jesus encounters at the hands of human beings the type of temptations to which he was exposed in the desert (Luke 4:1–11). Precisely because God's salvation is so revolutionary in its promise and expectation, it invites counter-response. Repentance does not come easy. It is a shocking experience.

From the Tyranny of Things

At the top of the list of tyrannical forces is the despotic power of things. Well aware of their potential for exploitation, Luke's Jesus issues constant warnings against measuring one's worth in denarii and drachmas. The rich fool was not stupid because he took thought for the future, but because he planned on a future without God in it and thought that he was in charge of that future. But without God he had no identity except that of a "fool." To top it off, he spoke his own epitaph while he was alive. The customary one ran: "Eat, drink, and be merry, for tomorrow you will be dead." This man hoped to give death the lie: "Eat, drink, and be merry, for the future is yours." Before the day was out in which he planned his bigger barns, he saw his wording changed.

A rich ruler found Jesus' liberating technique shocking (18:18–23). Luke says that he went away very sorrowful. Repentance would have spelled joy, as it did for Zacchaeus (19:6), who could not wait to pay the price for his shock therapy.

To Luke the tyranny of things is not only a threat to personal identity, but the source of much social exploitation. Luke also recognized that societies most penetrated by elements of traditional religion can be the most exploitative. This combination of political-economic power with religious sanction is well-nigh irresistible, for there exists endemic opposition to change. In his report of Paul's difficulty with the silver trade at Ephesus, Luke exposed Demetrius who supported preservation of "our jobs" with the desperate plea that these newcomers were taking their deity Artemis away from them (Acts 19:23–40). In Acts 16:16–24 Luke shows how a woman reputed to be psychic was exploited for gain.

Similar exposure of an unholy alliance between religious and material interests takes place in Luke 20:45–47. Practiced legal experts could through perennial updating steer traditional law in the direction of personal economic profit. Sensitive to this fact, Luke unmasks those who improve their estates with prayer as a front. Being a part of his proclamation, the inclusion of such a story in his work is a perennial call to repentance. As power structures in society, religious groups sometimes find it shocking even to consider repentance for the ways in which God's rule is affirmed in word, but its power denied in deed. The same applies to phony revolutionary structures that promise liberation and project a perpetual apocalyptic program of periodic plans that aggrandize privileged revolutionaries while suppressing critique from the faceless masses.

From the Tyranny of
Social Class

Jesus lost no time in challenging the importance of conforming to group pressures, and he aimed to break the grip of those who through inherited social patterns and accompanying prejudices deprived humanity of all real personal identity. Through his own adoption of a slave's role Jesus identified with humanity at the lowest social level. And by reinforcing Jesus' role as Master (Acts 2:36) God upended all pride in class, except that of being a faithful slave to the Master of all. With the name of Jesus, God served notice on all present and future claimants to power that Jesus' claims took precedence over any other claims to obedience of human beings. It was a liberated people, with fresh perspective on authority, who said, "Our first allegiance must be to God, not to human beings" (Acts 5:29). Peter uses the word *dei* (it is necessary), a word that Luke uses in his Gospel to describe much of Jesus' decisive activity. When the religious establishment tried to censor their references to Jesus of Nazareth, Peter and John replied, "You are authorities on whether one ought to listen to God ahead of human beings. In any case, we can't be silent about what we have seen and heard" (Acts 4:19–20). This was dynamic interpretation of the incident recorded in Luke 20:19–26.

A second instrument of despotic darkness is the tyranny of class and caste. Unlike Paul, who considered most of the data of Jesus' life uninteresting for Christian faith and morals, Luke attaches great importance to Jesus' words and actions, for in them are revealed a pattern for all varieties of Christian decision. Encouragement to imitate benefactors is a common theme in Greco-Roman public decrees. As the Great Benefactor, Jesus is eminently worthy of such imitation. And the life of the apostolic church is a partial commentary on how the life of Jesus can be meaningfully integrated with the daily demands for such decisions. Basic to such discipline is the commitment expressed in Acts 4:19–20, a commitment that is generated by the directive of Jesus in Luke 20:25 and reinforced by Jesus' own approach to tyrannical social structures and forces. The "right" cause (Acts 4:19, *dikaion*) is at issue.

In the course of capsizing the whole system of classification of righteous and unrighteous, Jesus even dared to tamper with definitions of the word "neighbor," and on one occasion embarrassed a legal expert by getting him to admit that a Samaritan could know more than a priest or a Levite about neighborliness (Luke 10:25–37). At another time he put a Pharisee down and elevated a publican (18:9–14). And at a dinner party he embarrassed a Pharisee before his guests and then pronounced absolution on a woman of questionable reputation (7:36–50).

In his attack on social stratification, Jesus also undermined traditions that kept women in their place. Israel could boast of some outstanding women leaders, and Rome had given women more recognition than had some other cultures, but Luke's Jesus appeared to go beyond the standard social practices. To be sure, there were no women called to be apostles, but he did not hesitate to be found frequently in their company (8:1–3; cf. 23:27, 49). In Luke's stories, women often outperform men (e.g., 7:36–50). Without them an important link of witnesses for the burial of Jesus would have been lost (Luke 23:55–56; 24:1–11). Together with the apostles a number of women gathered in an upper room after Jesus' ascension to await the will of God (Acts 1:14). Saul of Tarsus learned that Christian women did not readily back off from his "threatening and slaughter," and his jails were seeing more and more of these courageous witnesses (see Acts 8:3; 9:2).

Is the Ethic Practical?

To cite further evidence of Jesus' radical confrontation of accepted economic and social patterns would most certainly stimulate protest that such an ethic is totally impractical. But the criticism dare not be lightly dismissed. It is one thing to utter fantastic words about a world one would like to have, but which does not actually exist, and another to offer guidance and direction in securing an improvement in the situation. The latter requires awareness of things as they are.

It is, of course, a truism that institutions find it difficult enough to hear cherished views and long established practices questioned, but seldom can they tolerate an invitation to repentance for the same. Belief in the infallibility and autonomy of one's own social-economic-political-religious inheritance is so deeply entrenched that defensive measures are quickly taken against anyone who calls it into question. Well aware of these facts, Luke deals with them in terms of the obligations of the leaders and of the led in an endeavor to answer the basic question: "At what level in the face of institutional patterns can individual identity emerge in such a way that the institution or group can make its optimum contribution to humanity?" This way of putting the question permits dissolution of the faceless entity into live components.

Responsibility for Liberation

Since groupness promotes security, the individual finds the self at a deep level of fear and anxiety in the face of change. Precisely at this point the relationship between leader(s) and led is crucial.

Responsibility of the Leaders. Leaders can deal with fear and anxiety in various ways. One way is to develop what may appear at first sight an even tighter sense of group identity by heavier bombardment of the enemy sectors, namely, any ideologies, programs, or practices that can be shown to conflict with the core ethos of the group. Those who take this tack will find ready allies. For example, Demetrios, manufacturer of souvenirs for visitors to the temple of Artemis at Ephesos, put his entire city into an uproar when he incited his craftspeople to protect the honor of their deity in the face of Paul's proclamation. They were, of course, aware of the potential loss of revenue and for two hours cried out with the crowd that had gathered for an irregular town meeting, "Great is Artemis of Ephesos" (Acts 19:34). In contrast to the rabble-rousing rhetoric of Demetrios is the approach of an unnamed city clerk, who also appealed to group sensitivities, but with his common sense succeeded in putting an end to the riot. First he pointed out that Artemis was too great a deity to suffer any dimunition of prestige. He then reminded the Ephesians that they were subjects of Rome and that the imperial establishment would take a dim view of unauthorized assemblies, not to speak of rioting (vv. 35–40). Of special interest in this same connection is the clerk's appraisal of the manners exhibited by Paul and his associates: "They are no pillagers of temples and they do not speak disparagingly of our deity" (v. 37). His judgment reflects the character of Paul's opening remarks at Athens: "I perceive in more ways than one that you are very religious" (17:22).

Luke is well aware of the existence of historical complexes that are more than the sum total of the human individuals involved. The governed and those who govern, in whatever capacity, are in a way inextricably intertwined. Yet the individual has responsibility to respond to the message of salvation, for the proclamation derives from the King of all the earth. In the Book of Acts, leaders of the people are especially called to account (Acts 4:25–28), for leaders are continually exposed to the temptation to deprive the led of their identity (Luke 22:25; Acts 20:30) and set up personality cults. Jesus himself was exposed to that temptation, but he overcame it successfully (Luke 4:1–11), and he became a servant of all (22:26). Therefore, leaders are to be called to repentance and to the obligation to recognize that their talents as leaders are gifts of a beneficent Creator to relieve the lot of the oppressed and "to set at liberty" (*aposteilai*) the captives enchained by social patterns, custom, and economic necessity (cf. 4:18–19). Religious leaders especially need to be called to repentance, lest they identify their interest in administrative tidiness and control of the group with God's interests (see Luke 12:41–48). Among the secular authorities whom Paul invited to faith in Jesus Christ were Procurator Felix (Acts 24:10–21) and King Agrippa (26:2–29).

Responsibility of the Led. But now it is the turn of those who are led. They also need to repent, for the gospel is no slogan of "Down with the rich, up with the poor." The Sermon on the Plain (Luke 6:17–49) turned to red any green light the Magnificat might have seemed to give to transference of the means of production. Also the poor, the hungry, the oppressed, and the persecuted are among those who are to "hear" (6:27) what Jesus has to say. The first thing he liberated them from is the thought that a mere redistribution of goods will solve their problems. Poor they may be, but like the rich they are to "lend, without expecting anything in return" (6:35). It is easy to lose the main thread here—both the power structure, the rich, and those who consider themselves out of it are called to repentance, that is, to be liberators. The rich are to reevaluate their power over the lives and happiness of others. The less rich are not to seek how quickly they can put others in their debt. On the contrary, they have the responsibility of being liberated so that they too can become liberators. Repentance of the love of slavery; repentance of the fear of speaking words of power to power; repentance of slavish adherence to tradition; repentance of all that satisfies one for the moment but forges chains for others who come after—this is the implication of Jesus' proclamation. The obligation to be free is part of the message of the radical gospel of the New Age.

There are, then, no exceptions. Repentance for liberation with a view to engaging in the task of liberation applies across the board. To document that fact, Luke presented John the Baptist's message as a comprehensive model. To the crowds he said, "One who has two shirts should give one to the person who doesn't have any. Do the same with your food." To tax-brokers he said, "Don't exact more than you're supposed to." Soldiers were given the answer: "No shakedowns, no blackmail!" These were all invitations to a revolution of lifestyle. Throughout, Luke sees the Great Benefactor at work in making benefactors out of all who come in contact with him, personally or through the Christian proclamation. Included, among others, are the women mentioned in Luke 8:1-3, the post-Pentecost sharing community (Acts 2:42-47; 4:32-35), generous Tabitha (9:36-39), and hospitable Lydia (16:14-15).

Is the Ethic Codified?

At first sight, Luke's statements on what constitutes moral and ethical behavior would appear disappointing. But mere proof-texting of what Luke considers proper performance is a grossly inadequate method of apprehending his thought. Performance of what is morally acceptable to God does not first of all begin in Christian existence. God takes careful note of the prayer and almsgiving of the non-Jew and non-Christian Cornelius (Acts 10:31). Like his counterpart in Luke 7:1-10, he is a benefactor, and like Zachariah and Elizabeth (Luke 1:5-6) he is "righteous" (*dikaios*, Acts 10:22). In another case, a Samaritan becomes a model for a ruler in Israel (Luke 10:25-37). Jesus declares that he has not come to call the righteous (*dikaioi*) but sinners to repentance (Luke 5:32; 15:7). How then are we to account for the paucity of specific directives, including very little reference even to love?

As was observed above, repentance is for Luke a revolution of the mind, and not necessarily and only a change from sin to virtue. The Christian proclamation is a call to recognize that all systems of the world are now under the mastery of Jesus Christ and that within those systems the prior authority of Jesus Christ is to be recognized. All are called to liberation, either from the temptation to dominance or from the temptation to servility, or from both, depending on the circumstances. According to Luke, people are to recognize that Satan endeavors with a counter-revolutionary claim to swindle humanity into serving him. The Christian proclamation exposes that scheme and calls for repentance; that is, it speaks against participation in such counter-revolutionary activity and for acceptance of the Lordship of Jesus Christ.

Mosaic Law

From such perspective Luke approaches the question of the validity of laws, ordinances, and social customs that give to human institutions historical integrity. For Christians in the latter half of the first century, and especially after the fall of Jerusalem, the question of their relation to Mosaic Law would loom large. With his emphasis on the preeminent authority of the name of Jesus, Luke shows that even God has taken a fresh turn with respect to legal and social structures documented in the OT and in subsequent tradition up to the time of Jesus. By throwing the divine lot in with the name of Jesus, God uses executive privilege to declare that the life and words of Jesus and the guidance of the Spirit take precedence over any prior ordinances. Thereby the old is preserved for whatever it is worth, the future is given carte blanche, and society is offered the possibility of functioning without total fracture. It is the politics of the New Age.

Luke's account of a conference in Jerusalem (Acts 15) shows how it all works, but a fair reflection of Luke's thinking on the matter is at hand in Luke 18:18–27. In this story Jesus himself recites traditional Mosaic commandments. The ruler is satisfied that he has kept these, and he is not challenged on that score. But then he is invited to a revolutionary course of action—"Sell all that you have and give the proceeds to the poor, and then associate yourself with me." Without his possessions he would have no visible evidence to verify his moral credentials. Moreover, by associating with Jesus he would be invited to life in which his own moral standards would be called into question as one who was a friend of publicans and sinners. In other words, Moses is not renounced, but more creative possibilities of moral existence are available to the one who is liberated from dependence on the code to which one has been accustomed. "From my youth," the ruler said (v. 21). But now the future called for erasure of all pride in past achievement.

Similarly, from the lawyer who asked how he might inherit life, Jesus elicited a response out of Deuteronomy and assured his questioner that performance would spell life (Luke 10:25–37). But only liberation for creative possibility would make possible such performance. One cannot codify all the possibilities of neighborly behavior. Instead, one must think in terms of being a neighbor, even as God is the benefactor of humanity. This means developing sensitivity to needs to be met. In a society such as yours, Luke would say to people in the West, given your political responsibilities under constitutional law, Christians are especially responsible, individually and collectively, for discovering ways and means of relieving the oppressed and setting free the prisoners who are caught in social and economic squirrel cages not of their own making. For, as Luke is careful to note, the Samaritan does not merely throw a few denarii at the feet of the beaten-up traveler. He moves the social machinery around him to effect recovery for the poor man, and he is prepared to check on the treatment! Luke leaves other creative possibilities open—such as improving protection for travelers on Jericho Road.

Secular Law and Order

Luke's apparently preferential treatment of Roman authorities for apologetic reasons is such a truism in studies of Luke-Acts that his interest in the ethical factor is largely ignored. The evangelist is at pains to point out that before their conversion to Jesus Christ, non-Jews may act in a manner very acceptable to God. Cornelius is described in language closely resembling the description of Zechariah and Elizabeth, and Joseph of Arimathea (Acts 10:2; see Luke 1:6; 23:50). God has taken special notice of his prayer and his almsgiving (v. 31). And Peter affirms that in "any nation, one who fears God and does what is right, is approved by God" (v. 35); that is, God does not demand conformity to specific ritual requirements, such as circumcision, for validation within the covenant made with Abraham. Thus the good news cleared the way for a nontribal and nonnationalistic approach to the worship of God. Sergius Paulus, governor of the island of Salamis, was, Luke tells us, a "prudent" person (Acts 13:7). The reason for Luke's description is apparent; the man wanted to hear the word of God. All this is in continuity with recitals in the Gospel. The centurion in Luke 7:1–10 is praised by Jewish authorities because he "loves our people and even built a synagogue for us," and also by Jesus for his faith that exceeded anything found in Israel. A Samaritan shows up a priest and a Levite (10:30–37). Another Samaritan, healed of leprosy, returns to Jesus and gives thanks, whereas nine others ignore their Benefactor (17:11–17). Goodness, Luke implies, is to be appreciated and encouraged wherever it is found, and God's long-standing adherents do not have a monopoly on it.

On the level of societal structures Luke shows that Roman officials are in the main very conscious about justice. Three times Pilate finds Jesus "not guilty" (23:4, 14, 22), and a Roman centurion declares Jesus "innocent." Luke makes the point especially through the rhetorical device of comparison with the performance of Jewish authorities, who naturally pride themselves on the loftier revelation given them through Moses. Not only did Jerusalem's authorities commit a grave crime in helping to condemn an innocent man, but instead of improving government they contributed to its deterioration by putting political pressure on Pilate to destroy Jesus when he was inclined to let him go (Acts 2:13–14; see Luke 23:25). Given their long traditions of justice, Jews ought to know better, argues Luke. Rome tries to keep peace, but some Jews try to prevent other Jews from proclaiming the name of Jesus, and then the authorities must step in. This happened with special notoriety at Thessalonika (Acts 17:5–9), at Corinth (18:12–17), and in Jerusalem (Acts 21—23). In the last two incidents Roman authorities distinguished themselves for their fairness.

On the other hand, Luke is critical of political tradeoffs involving people's lives, for the very purpose of government is to sustain an orderly society and to protect the interests of the weak against the encroachments of the powerful, and Christians have a special responsibility to help keep their officials honest. Three examples stand out in the Book of Acts. Herod (Agrippa I) had James the brother of John killed, and this so pleased his constituency that he planned to use Peter as an encore (Acts 12:1-3). Similarly, Felix is indicted by Luke for using Paul to pay off political debts (24:27). And Paul lets Festus know that he was not about to be the governor's political tool. Therefore he appealed to Nero (25:11), the ultimate arbiter of Rome's constitution.

There is nothing like public demonstrations to test politicians' spines for their sponge point. The magistrates at Philippi gave in before public pressure, and Paul spent part of the night in jail. After a slight tremor, Paul converted his jailer and at daybreak was told by representatives of the authorities that he and Silas were free to leave the prison—which by now was minimum security anyway. They were also urged to depart from the city, a request that Paul refused. Having saved his ace for the right moment, he asked whether the authorities were now going to add smuggling of prisoners to their crime of flogging innocent Roman citizens. "No," he said, "we want an escort, right out the front gate!" (Acts 16:35-40). In effect, Paul is displayed in Acts 16 as one who compliments Rome for its sense of equity, which permitted citizens to rebuke local officials without fear of reprisal.

Power must retain integrity, says Luke, and Christians are obligated to contribute to its preservation. Justice has a high calling and no one can permit its prostitution to low motive. This approach is a far cry from the quiescent attitude toward authority, secular or ecclesiastical, that has been so frequently encouraged, sometimes under the rubric of two kingdoms.

Much more might be said about Luke's contributions to a theology of ethics, but sufficient data have been explored to demonstrate the importance of the subject for Luke. What at first sight seems a weakness is one of the strengths in his presentation. Since his ethical perspective includes the positive contributions of the various cultures and systems of this world, and since he assumes that Christians function within the context of such cultures and systems, he does not envisage a specifically Christian ethical system to which all humanity might one day subscribe.

All this does not mean Luke merely espouses good citizenship. A specific social group may give its citizenship award for the year to the citizen who best exemplifies the traditions and standards of the group. But at the end of that route rises the high altar of the god called status quo. Rather, Luke presupposes for Christian existence a revolution of the mind that prepares one to be a catalyst for change in the creative enterprise of exploring the needs of one's fellow human beings. In effect, he advances the process of democratizing the Mediterranean concept of personal excellence that manifested itself in civic responsibility. In the modern day this means that precisely because Christians relate to a God who brings salvation in history, they cannot retreat from the issues of poverty, majority-minority conflict, sexism, human justice, and other problems that involve commitment to avowed constitutional objectives.

Through his view of two-phase apocalyptic, with emphasis on the name of Jesus, Luke solidified Christians' contact with their world. And by virtue of the fact that this same Jesus is the judge of all the earth, the Christian can never be claimed by any status quo.

Ethics Rooted in Christology

It might be objected that eschatology of a kind now outmoded has qualified Luke's ethic to such a degree that the ethic itself is meaningless apart from the eschatological presuppositions of his age. But Luke's christologizing of popular apocalyptic, as well as his historicizing of it through the life of Jesus, protects his ethics against such charges of discontinuity and irrelevance. In Luke it is not the eschatological expectation of the judgment that motivates Christian ethics. The "downstroke" of God's axe anticipated by John never did come. Luke knows that well. But in another way it came down hard, for any society that does not heed the call to salvation through self-criticism, through invitation to creative social enterprise, through courageous refusal to encourage and accept anything but the best out of authorities, civilian or public, will not have to wait for the end of the world. Like the rich fool, it will learn, "Tonight you may no longer be steward." History may go on, but whose will these things be? Luke is primarily interested in positive motivation, and he roots it in his Christology.

Jesus as the Son of God is the obedient Israelite, but he sums up in his life a creative approach to inherited law. He refused to bow down before the altar of status quo. He found his own ethical unity in obedience to his heavenly Parent's purpose, defined as creative awareness and response to the possibilities of mercy. That diluted the power of conflicting claims on his loyalty. Faith in Jesus means that one accepts the verdict of God not only on the innocence of Jesus (he is *dikaios*), but also on the validity of his obedience, which brought him into creative conflict with his traditions. The story of the apostolic church is the story of continuation of what Jesus began to do and to teach, for all Christians, like Israel of old, are the slaves of one Master. For Luke ecclesiology is of a piece with Christology, and ethics is inextricably connected with that Christology. There is no room in his thinking for religiosity or citizenship that are socially neutral or apathetic.

But how do such findings hold up in the light of a test case such as Luke's sequence of the story of the Good Samaritan and the story of Mary and Martha (Luke 10:29–42)? There seems to be here an irreconcilable ethical conflict between a call to action and the praise of inaction. It is imperative therefore to take into account the social context implied by the narrative. In the case of 10:38–42, Luke maintains continuity with Jesus' extraordinary approach to social tradition. Martha, in keeping with Eastern hospitality, reflects the customary lavish expenditure of time and effort on the guest. This involves her in recriminations. Moreover, she is actually insulting to her guest, asking him to give orders to her sister, whom she views, along with herself, as a slave in the situation. Along with Luke's integration of this story with his treatment elsewhere of Jesus' critique of social traditions, the evangelist pursues a christological motif. Martha is busy preparing a huge dinner, in her own way as a benefactor, for Jesus. But what she does not realize is that Jesus is in fact the host and the Great Benefactor, who on one occasion turned down the production of bread (4:1–11), yet produced it for others at the banquet of the five thousand (9:12–17). Jesus continues his "benefactions" through his followers. "You feed them," he said to the disciples in Galilee (9:13). After Pentecost, the needs of "about five thousand men" were met in another way (Acts 4:1–4; cf. Luke 9:14), and the people of God were equipped for appropriate action (cf. Acts 4:32–37).

Reappearing constantly in Luke's narrative is the thought, "Hear the word of God and keep it." Action without thought leads to much of the do-goodism from which society suffers. The ruler in Luke 10:25–37 was seeking direction for action that he had never thought of. With the subsequent story of Mary and Martha, Luke dramatically expressed back-to-back what might easily have become a theological cliche. Far from being in conflict, the two stories are rhetorically, theologically, and ethically coherent. Ultimately, Christians compose communities that back action within a strong context of critical theological awareness.

Summary

The following schematic exhibit will illustrate how multi-faceted Luke's Gospel is in its moral and ethical statement, with admonition, exhortation, and consolation in perceptive balance:

1. Jesus aims to liberate humanity from demeaning views of God.
   a. God is not a vengeful autocrat. God searches for the sinner and in connection with Jesus of Nazareth proclaims executive pardon to all people who return in repentance.
   b. God is no respecter of persons and makes no deal with anyone.
   c. God is no front for self-motivated religiosity.
   d. God is not at the beck and call of dogmatic and liturgical formulae.
   e. God affirms life, not death.
   f. God does not patronize people by excusing anyone from ultimate judgment. Those who *refuse* to be free *shall* not be free to share the King's banquet.

2. Jesus and his associates proclaim forgiveness and liberation from demeaning confinement.

a. Jesus simplified religion through elevation of mercy. He liberated theology from reduction to head trips.

b. Jesus challenged tyranny of tradition. He dared to touch innumerable sacred cows of ritual and social-political-economic custom that make people expendable and stratify in terms of competitive advantage.

c. Jesus challenged the view that ritual and human malady were incompatible. The Sabbath dawned each week so that salvation might become a reality on that day. Jesus had a genius for finding apocalyptic possibility in holy days.

d. Jesus challenged reciprocity systems that put justice and truth and quality of life at the mercy of personal or corporate profit and prestige.

e. Jesus refused to be intimidated. He spoke power to power and was passionately outraged against exploitation of the weak.

f. Jesus aimed to liberate leaders from cultivation of personality cult, and he discouraged his followers from encouraging such demonic self-interest.

g. Jesus liberated his followers from a sense of helplessness in the face of apparently invincible and immovable evil. He gave them personal identity through his invitation to enterprising moral choices. He encouraged freedom of speech that is prompted by the Holy Spirit and discouraged conversation which is dominated by restrictive traditional interests or societal patterns.

h. Jesus liberated people from the idea that the optimum was life without hazard and religion without pain. He reduced the conflicts of life to the possibility of sacrifice and magnificent service.

i. Jesus challenged provinciality and narrowness of mind.

j. Jesus liberated his followers from preoccupation with their own public image, for he himself endured ambiguity through identification with the concerns of the weak and the disenfranchised.

k. Jesus liberated his followers from the patronage that exploits in the interests of corporate advancement. He offered no cut-rate price for entrance into the kingdom. For example, toll collectors do not enter by thanking God they are not Pharisees.

l. Jesus liberated humanity from substandard instruments for measuring worth and offered identity to the individual above and beyond the accidents of history. He declared that ability to stand before the Son of humanity was all that mattered, thereby offering his followers regal command *over* history.

m. Jesus liberated his followers from fear and anxiety by encouraging a community of openness and trust.

n. Jesus liberated from a sense of moral superiority by leveling all his associates to the status of unprofitable slaves. Freed from self-aggrandizing bookkeeping, they were at liberty to be useful to people and to God.

o. Jesus liberated from the desire for power *over* others to greatness in the performance of benefactions *for* others.

p. Jesus liberated his followers for receipt of the Holy Spirit, the endowment for innovative performance in the New Age. A swept and garnished house filled with positive values would not tolerate an invasion of seven worse spirits led by the original tenant.

This list does not do justice to the length and breadth of Luke's moral and ethical thinking, but it does suggest further avenues for reflection on the two components of excellence that occupy his work, namely "piety" and "uprightness," each of which is part of a rich and complex semantic field in Luke-Acts.

It might, finally, be asked, how it is that with such emphasis on the theme of liberation neither the verb *eleutheroō* (free) nor the noun *eleutheria* (freedom) is to be found in all of Luke's work. The fact is that this word family would suggest liberation of domestic slaves and would promote misunderstanding among Luke's public. Luke denied himself the overt authorial privileges available to a writer of epistles. By avoiding these terms Luke is able to establish a broader base for his theme of liberation. Through his stress on crucifixion, a form of execution reserved especially for rebellious slaves and malefactors, he is able to establish contact with those on the lowest stratum of society. At that level all kingdom candidates must identify in order to qualify for exaltation.

Some comprehension of the social and political implications of such proclamation in the first century can be gained if one asks what might have happened in Germany if Christians had emerged from their churches with armbands identifying themselves as Jews. What lethal attacks might have been made against racism in the United States had its churches collectively identified with the experiences of Indians, blacks, and others. True ecumenism is realized when all followers of Jesus recognize themselves as slaves to the One Master and subjects of the King of kings. Through acknowledgment of that supremacy they evaluate all other claims, with the understanding that in case of conflict of loyalties the vote is to be cast for the Master of all. Thus all are liberated in a way that no official emancipation declaration of the world could free them. To be liberated for the task of making liberators of others is the highest privilege enjoyed by participants in the mission of Jesus, Great Servant and Benefactor.

NOTES

Chapter 1: Thought and Structure

1. W. Dittenberger, *Sylloge inscriptionum graecarum*, 3d ed., no. 797. Hereafter abbreviated *SIG³*.

2. The connotation "innocent" is secondary to "upright." See my *Benefactor*, 345–46.

Chapter 3: Exceptional Merit and Beneficence

1. Sources for the Greek text are cited in *Benefactor*, no. 33.

2. W. Dittenberger, *Orientis Graecae Inscriptiones Selectae*, no. 668. Hereafter abbreviated *OGI*.

3. *Benefactor*, 339–40.

4. *SIG³* 547.9–11.

5. *OGI* 532.11–12.

6. The participial form *euergetōn* functions as a substantive. The usage is common in inscriptions relating to benefactor.

7. For further discussion of the word-deed pair, see *Benefactor*, 339–43.

8. For detailed discussion of the Servant figure, see chap. 6 of this book. In his second installment, Luke has Paul and his co-workers function in a similar capacity as benefactors to the nations (Acts 13:47; cf. 26:18).

9. At Luke 4:40 the evangelist adds that Jesus laid his hands on the demon-possessed, but at v. 41 adds that he "rebuked" the demons.

10. *Benefactor*, no. 29.15, 43.

11. *Benefactor*, nos. 1–4.

12. These and other texts are cited in *Benefactor*, no. 28, with references to other miraculous healing in antiquity (pp. 193–96).

13. On attestation of benefactors' performance, see *Benefactor*, 442–47.

14. *SIG³* 762.38–39; *Benefactor*, no. 12.

15. For details on Menas, see *Benefactor*, no. 17.

16. Iamblichos *Pythagoras* 33.234–36.

17. Demades 4 [179].

18. Lysias 6.40; *Benefactor*, 417.

19. Other passages that include a reference to Jesus' beneficence and the hostile response that it elicits are Luke 5:17–26; 6:6–11; and 11:14–16.

20. *OGI* 532.15–18.

21. *Benefactor*, 259.

22. For further details and references, see my commentary on Luke 1; 23:44–49; 24:51–52 in *Jesus and the New Age*.

Chapter 4: Reversal of Fortunes

1. David Mamet, *The Chicago Tribune Magazine*, June 29, 1986, sec. 10, p. 7.
2. E. Diehl, *Anthologia Lyrica Graeca* (Teubner, 1925).
3. *Iliad* 19:287–90; see also in the *Iliad* the laments by Hekuba (22:431–36) and by Andromache (22:477–514).
4. Ludlul Bel Nemequi, Tablet II; trans. Lambert, p. 41, lines 39–42.
5. "The Desecration of the Han Tombs," trans. Arthur Wiley, *Translations from the Chinese* (New York, 1941), p. 76.

Chapter 5: Jesus—Christ and Lord

1. All apologetic debate to the contrary, 1 Esdras 5:5 is formally parallel to Luke's use of the proper name followed immediately by the specification of lineage and with detailed support for his ancestry given in the genealogy cited in Luke 3:23–38 (see also 2:4).
2. *Benefactor*, 423.

Chapter 6: Salvation and Repentance

1. Luke 5:26 contains the cognate *ekstasis* in a textually uncertain passage.
2. See also Deut. 31:27; Pss. 5:11[10]; 65[66]:7; 67:7[68:6]; 94[95]:8; 105[106]:7; Ezek. 3:9; 12:9.
3. The highlighting of Paul's role as Servant is one of the reasons for Luke's apparent disinterest in the careers of most of the other apostles.

SELECTED BIBLIOGRAPHY

Commentaries

For the General Reader

Danker, Frederick W. *Jesus and the New Age: A Commentary on St. Luke's Gospel.* 2d ed., revised and enlarged. Philadelphia: Fortress Press, 1987. Integrates the results of historical and literary criticism in relation to contemporary interest in structuralism and social context, with emphasis on the variety of literary and cultural influences functioning in Luke's thought and composition. It aims to assist the contemporary proclaimer and reader in recapturing the dramatic impact of the original as a coherent literary work.

Ellis, E. Earle. *The Gospel of Luke.* Rev. ed. New Century Bible. Grand Rapids: Wm. B. Eerdmans, 1974 (1966). Based on the Revised Standard Version. Ellis pays constant attention to the function of form in the communication of meaning. Besides comments on words and phrases, Ellis discusses each section under one or more of the following categories: structure, teaching, and background. Expert use of Hebrew-language sources enriches this exposition.

Karris, Robert J. *Invitation to Luke: A Commentary on the Gospel of Luke with Complete Text of the Jerusalem Bible.* Garden City, N.Y.: Doubleday & Co., 1977. Designed for individual and group Bible study.

Schweizer, Eduard. *The Good News According to Luke.* Trans. David E. Green. Atlanta: John Knox, 1984.

Talbert, Charles H. *Reading Luke: A Literary and Theological Commentary on the Third Gospel.* New York: Crossroad, 1982. Features understanding of Luke in historical and cultural context.

For the Advanced Student

Creed, J. M. *The Gospel According to St. Luke: The Greek Text with Introduction, Notes, and Indices.* London: Macmillan and Co., 1953 (1930).

Fitzmyer, Joseph A. *The Gospel According to Luke.* Anchor Bible Series, 28 and 28A. 2 vols. Garden City, N.Y.: Doubleday & Co., 1981, 1985.

Marshall, I. Howard. *The Gospel of Luke: A Commentary on the Greek Text.* The New International Greek Testament Commentary. Grand Rapids: Wm. B. Eerdmans, 1978.

Schürmann, H. *Das Lukasevangelium.* Erster Teil. Herders Theologischer Kommentar zum Neuen Testament. Band III. Freiburg: Herder, 1969. Only 1:1—9:50 has appeared.

Special Studies

These selected specialized studies of Luke's work will direct one to the vast body of literature available on Luke's two-volume work:

Brown, Schuyler. *Apostasy and Perseverance in the Theology of Luke.* Analecta Biblica 36. Rome: Pontifical Biblical Institute, 1969. Perceptive observations, especially on Luke's ethical perspective, with challenge to Conzelmann's understanding of "temptation."

Cadbury, Henry Joel. *The Making of Luke-Acts.* New York: Macmillan, 1927. A delightful study for the general reader, whom it takes into Luke's literary workshop. A classic in its own right. Cadbury's verdict of "general obscurity of plan" must be called into question, but much modern editorial criticism requires correction in view of his many insights and fertile observations well accompanied by sober judgment and fine historical discernment.

Cassidy, Richard J. *Jesus, Politics, and Society: A Study of Luke's Gospel.* Maryknoll, N.Y.: Orbis Books, 1978. Discusses the political and social stance of Jesus. For the general reader, with much supporting evidence.

Cassidy, Richard J., and Philip J. Scharper, eds. *Political Issues in Luke-Acts.* New York: Orbis Books, 1983. A series of ten essays by various scholars on political aspects of Luke's Gospel and the Book of Acts.

Conzelmann, Hans. *The Theology of St. Luke.* Trans. by G. Buswell. Philadelphia: Fortress Press, 1982 (1960). This English-language edition does not include the revisions available in the third German edition (Tübingen: J. C. B. Mohr, 1960). A partial correction of Cadbury's verdict, but especially deficient in assessment of the role of chaps. 1 and 2 in Luke's Gospel.

Danker, Frederick W. *Benefactor: Epigraphic Study of a Graeco-Roman and New Testament Semantic Field.* Clayton Publishing House, Box 9258, St. Louis, 1982. Translations of selected inscriptions open up for the general reader features of the political-religious-cultural arena in which Luke's Gospel took shape. The detailed notes and index to discussion of passages in Luke-Acts will aid the advanced student.

Ellis, E. Earle. *Eschatology in Luke.* Philadelphia: Fortress Press, 1972. A solid study, with bibliography, on one of the most disputed topics in Lukan research. See also John Reumann's introduction.

Farris, Stephen. *The Hymns of Luke's Infancy Narratives.* Sheffield, Eng.: JSOT Press, 1985. A technical discussion of the origin, meaning, and significance of the hymns in Luke 1 and 2.

Flender, Helmut. *St. Luke: Theologian of Redemptive History.* Trans. by R. H. and I. Fuller. Philadelphia: Fortress Press, 1967. In critique of Conzelmann, Flender stresses the exaltation of Jesus as the consummation of salvation in heaven.

Jervell, Jacob. *Luke and the People of God: A New Look at Luke-Acts.* Minneapolis: Augsburg, 1972. One of the best resources for exploring the question of Israel's rejection of the gospel as depicted by Luke.

Keck, Leander E., J. Louis Martyn, eds. *Studies in Luke-Acts.* Philadelphia: Fortress Press, 1980 (1966). A series of classic essays by seventeen scholars.

Kingsbury, Jack Dean. *Jesus Christ in Matthew, Mark, and Luke.* Proclamation Commentaries. Philadelphia: Fortress Press, 1981. A highly prized nontechnical discussion of Luke's Christology. See chap. 4 especially.

Krodel, Gerhard. *Acts*. Proclamation Commentaries. Philadelphia: Fortress Press, 1981. Luke's Gospel should not be read in isolation from Acts, and Krodel offers the general reader a guide to the evangelist's second volume. Included is a bibliography for the study of Acts.

O'Toole, Robert F. *The Unity of Luke's Theology: An Analysis of Luke-Acts*. Wilmington, Del.: Michael Glazier, 1984. A popular discussion of the dominant threads that go into Luke's literary tapestry.

Pilgrim, Walter E. *Good News for the Poor*. Minneapolis: Augsburg, 1981. For the general reader. Points to a new vision of intelligent discipleship in caring community.

Tiede, David L. *Prophecy and History in Luke-Acts*. Philadelphia: Fortress Press, 1980. Nontechnical, but for advanced students of Luke's work. A perceptive study of the roots of Christian faith in God's purpose as displayed in the Old Testament.

INDEX